He Never Came Home

He Never Came Home

Interviews, Stories, and Essays from Daughters
on Life Without Their Fathers

EDITED BY Regina R. Robertson

BOLDEN

AN AGATE IMPRINT

CHICAGO

Printed in the United States of America

He Never Came Home
ISBN 13: 978-1-932841-99-2 (trade paper)
ISBN 10: 1-932841-99-7 (trade paper)
eISBN 13: 978-1-57284-797-2
eISBN 10: 1-57284-797-2
First edition: June 2017

10 9 8 7 6 5 4 3 2 1   17 18 19 20 21

Bolden Books is an imprint of Agate Publishing. Agate books are
available in bulk at discount prices. Learn more at agatepublishing.com.

for

Jeanette G. Farnell,
my Groggy,
who named me and loved me more than I ever understood.
I miss you, every day.
I live and write to make you proud.

Ms. Butler,
who was always a strong voice and presence,
thank you for sharing your story, first.

and
my mother, my everything,
Valerie Regina,
for, well . . . everything, every time, always.

Contents

Foreword JOY-ANN REID ix

Introduction 1

PART I: DISTANT

The Birthday Present NIKO AMBER 9

Who Is My Father?
  DEMETREA HARDIMAN, AS TOLD TO THE EDITOR 15

Again DANIELLE RENE 23

A Lesson from My Mother NICOLE SHEALEY 31

My Sugar Pie DESNEY BUTLER, AS TOLD TO THE EDITOR............ 39

Here and There SIMONE I. SMITH, AS TOLD TO THE EDITOR 49

The Girl at the Window SARAH TOMLINSON 59

I Was the Different One
  NISA RASHID, AS TOLD TO THE EDITOR 69

PART II: DIVORCED

What's in a Name?
  TAMALA MERRITT, AS TOLD TO THE EDITOR 75

Redefining Family REGINA KING, AS TOLD TO THE EDITOR 81

Love, Peace, and Happiness . . . Despite My Father
  CINDY M. BIRCH 89

The Friendly Demon KYRA GROVES 101

He Always Said, "I Love You"
TRESA L. SANDERS, AS TOLD TO THE EDITOR 107

All Is Forgiven CORI MURRAY 119

Every Time You Go Away ALYSSE ELHAGE...................131

PART III: DECEASED

My Daddy's Girl, Still KIRSTEN WEST SAVALI 145

Going There JENNY LEE............... 153

You Did It Your Way BRIDGETTE BARTLETT ROYALL.................. 163

Life, After
MAI HUGGINS LASSITER, AS TOLD TO THE EDITOR 167

That Day in April WENDY L. WILSON................... 175

The Way It Should Be
GABRIELLE REECE, AS TOLD TO THE EDITOR.........................181

Death of a Stranger REGINA R. ROBERTSON 189

Acknowledgments 201

About the Contributors 205

About the Editor 209

Foreword

BY JOY-ANN REID

How do you mourn something that never was? That central question permeates *He Never Came Home*, in which Regina R. Robertson and her contributors walk through the pain, dislocation, and in some cases, the numbness that fatherless daughters feel. The essays within this collection are gripping: tragic, triumphant, and authentic. And they reveal the special hurt that a daughter knows when she is denied that first, innocent flash of true love.

But this book is more complex than even that.

Grappling with the loss of a once-present and beloved father-teacher, as Kirsten West Savali does in beautiful measure in "My Daddy's Girl, Still"; or coming to grips with the ache of constant disappointment, empty promises, and deliberate absence, as in "The Girl at the Window" by Sarah Tomlinson; or with the cyclical, generational dislocation caused by divorce, as Regina King recounts in "Redefining Family," *He Never Came Home* traverses the range of emotions that grip the fatherless daughter.

I was drawn into this project after writing a long essay on Facebook about the death of my own father, a swashbuckling, leather jacket–clad, Spider-sports-car-driving, intellectual gadfly who wooed my mother during some mysterious period in the early 1960s. The two of them came together in Iowa (of all places) from the distant shores of London, by way of Georgetown, Guyana, in the case of my mother, and the newly liberated Democratic Republic of the Congo, in that of my father. How they each wound up in America, or together, or producing one daughter in Des Moines, another in Brooklyn, and a son in Denver, all of whom my father swiftly, and to our minds, casually abandoned, on his way to more wives—some simultaneously—and many more children, I'll never know. Both my parents are gone, and my mother, who passed away when I was seventeen, was as tight-lipped about her past as she was fierce in her independence. Brilliant, creative, and resilient, she was a struggling single mom who was still adventurous in traversing the country, three kids in tow, in a Chevy station wagon.

That Facebook essay provoked an overwhelming response, as friends and coworkers, strangers, and even family members who had their own vague, distant memories of my father flooded me with emotional responses that veered between condolence and that wispy void where condolences don't seem quite right, but you just don't know what else to say.

Not knowing much about your father other than that he abandoned you, made occasional appearances fraught with high drama, abused your sister, drew tears from your baby brother, and elicited a mix of anxiety and pity, doesn't make mourning him any less complicated. But as the women who share their stories in this book reveal, how that loss shapes you depends less on the substance of the man who's gone away or on his manner of leaving—whether through addiction and self-harm, or suicide, or apparent uninterest, or the unyielding, icy authority of mortal disease—and more on what the loss created in the mourner: in some cases, resilience; in others, self-doubt; in still others, a determination to move on and to be whole, regardless.

This is an important book that will heal many hearts, impart the occasional stream of tears, and most importantly, give meaning and acknowledgement to an experience too many of us share: the loss of a natural and irreplaceable love every child truly deserves.

JOY-ANN (JOY) REID is the host of the show *A.M. Joy* on MSNBC and the author of *Fracture: Barack Obama, the Clintons, and the Racial Divide* (William Morrow/Harper Collins).

Introduction

IN ALL HONESTY, I've been writing this book forever. Long before I discovered my love of words, I was writing this book.

My mother raised me on her own, from day one. She's the only parent I've ever had. My father was never in the picture—not for one second, minute, or hour. I never met him. There were times when I wondered how a man could leave his family, his *kid*, and not look back, but I didn't obsess over my father's absence. I definitely thought about it, though.

I thought about how detached one must feel to just up and leave. But on the flip side, I always had a very clear understanding of the fact that people do what they want to do and stick around for who and what they want to stick around for. I'm pretty certain that those feelings were born from being abandoned by one of my parents. To me, the whys and the hows didn't really matter. I'm not sure how much they do now, either. Life goes on, and you've got to keep moving. That's the black and white of it, of course, but life has a way of showing you that the gray areas count for something, too.

Back in January 2001, I was in quite a state. For the first time in my life, I'd been fired from a job, one that I hated with every fiber of my being. In no time, my severance check dwindled to pennies, and I was having some serious concerns about how my rent would get paid.

It was during those first days and weeks of being unemployed that I started asking myself what I really wanted to do before paying bills became my sole motivation for getting out of bed each morning. I thought about the things I'd daydreamed about as a kid. First, I wanted to be a nurse (actually, I just wanted to care for newborns in the maternity ward), then I wanted to be a model and a dancer and an ad executive, and so on. I was always reading, and as much as I loved books, magazines were my real lifeline, so I thought about starting there. Eventually, I decided to take a leap and try my hand at modeling and writing. It was an idea I'd been toying with for years, so I figured I'd try them both and see which one stuck. I had nothing, and everything, to lose, so if the rent was going to be late anyway, I thought I might as well bet on myself.

I spent the next year and a half zigzagging between my adopted city of Los Angeles and my home base of New York, trying to catch the ever-elusive interest of modeling agents and magazine editors. I made some leads, had a few photo shoots, and even nabbed a couple of tear sheets, but in the end, the modeling didn't pan out. Just as I was approaching the crossroads of broke and terrified, I got the number of a friend of a friend who worked in the ad sales department of *Honey* magazine. He was supportive from the jump. In a matter of days, we met at the front desk, and he walked me over to the editorial side with a pat on the back and an endorsement that would kick off my writing career. When I asked the features editor what types of stories she was looking for and what I should write about, she told me, simply, "Write what you know." And that's what I did. My first national feature was entitled "Where's Daddy?"

The story ran in October 2002, and I was truly beside myself when the magazine hit newsstands. I didn't tell *my* story, though.

Instead, I interviewed a psychologist, an author, and three women, the latter of whom had each grown up without their fathers. I felt accomplished, but I never had any expectations beyond the possibility of writing my *next* feature story. I wasn't thinking about who might read that story or recognize my byline, so I was surprised by the feedback I received from my friends and colleagues. The question I heard most often was, "Why didn't you think to interview me?"

Until I'd signed the contract to write the article, I was under the illusion that this was my story alone. My father not being around wasn't something I ever really talked about. I thought it was embarrassing, and at one time in my life, his absence felt like a reflection of me. I remember wondering, "How horrible a person must you be for your father not to care about you?" Yes, that is embarrassing, but again, I thought it was just me. Writing that article made me realize that my upbringing wasn't unique, that I wasn't special—not in the least bit. That's when the idea of crafting a book, *this* book, came to mind.

As the years passed and writing features and cover stories became a full-time thing, I put the book idea on the back burner. Then I would pick it up, and put it back—over and over again. While I was figuring out how to turn the idea into a possibility, I thought about other fatherless women, those whose fathers weren't there for other reasons. There were women whose relationships with their fathers had been altered after their parents' divorce or separation. Then there were those who lost their fathers to illness, prison, or violence. Though their circumstances were different, they were dealing with issues of loss. Their stories needed to be told, too.

When I started my research for the book proposal, I discovered a statistic, courtesy of the National Fatherhood Initiative and the United States Census Bureau, which suggests that 24 million children in the United States under the age of 18 are being raised in a household without a biological father present. No, I definitely wasn't alone. Statistics are what they are, though. They're informational, sure, but they can't speak to the emotions that are tied to the experience. And everybody's experience is different.

As I was writing and editing this book, I lamented over the idea that I could waste any amount of precious brain power on someone who wasn't there, when my mother—the person who'd stuck by me and was down for me—was *still* holding me down. It wasn't until I read Barack Obama's book *Dreams from My Father* that I realized, again, that I was not alone. In his preface to the 2004 edition, former President Obama, who, sadly, lost his mother soon after the book's initial release in 1995, referenced the possibly of having written a different book, one that was "less a meditation on the absent parent, more a celebration of the one who was the single constant in my life." Right? *Right.*

Growing up without a father used to be my silent shame, but I'm now wise enough to know that it is a small part of who I am. It took many years for me to accept that. I've also learned to accept the fact that people are placed in your life—or not—for a reason. If things had worked out differently, perhaps I wouldn't be the woman or the writer I am today.

Every step leads you to the next, and I can now see how much my experiences led me here, to a space where I can share my story. So yes, I've been writing this book forever. Even when the idea was warming on the back burner for all of those years, I knew that I'd eventually get to the business of putting pen to paper, fingertips to keyboard, and speaking the truth. And I have, finally, along with twenty-one other courageous women.

This collection of essays is for all of the fatherless girls and women who've ever thought, as I once did, that a piece of them was missing. It's so important to understand that you have *you*. And as Glinda the Good Witch once said, "You've always had the power, my dear. You've had it all along."

Life has taught me that no matter the circumstances you're born into, you are responsible for steering your ship. If I can do it, you can, too . . . and you will. It just takes time.

REGINA R. ROBERTSON

I. Distant

The Birthday Present

NIKO AMBER

H E PLACED THE GIFT ON THE TABLE next to our food. It was flawlessly wrapped, with every crease of paper folded at a perfect angle and a bow placed carefully on top. I could tell that he hadn't wrapped it himself, not only because of the immaculate presentation, but also because the paper was decorated with the Barnes & Noble logo.

The present was large, about the size of an encyclopedia. My thirteenth birthday was last month, and he had been texting my mom about giving it to me for weeks. I quickly ripped open the paper, curiosity taking over. Inside, I found a thick book about astrology. I stared at the cover and tried to hide my emotions. I knew that if I caught his eye, the disappointment would show on my face. As I looked more closely at the book jacket, I noticed it was illustrated with sketches of naked people. I quickly glanced away, embarrassed. Suddenly the table we were sitting at seemed too small for the two of us.

"I knew you'd love it!" he said in his low, gravelly voice.

"Right," I replied. "This is nice."

The truth is, I'm not at all interested in astrology. I didn't like the book, especially the cover, but how would he know that? My father knows nothing about me. He only sees me once a year.

I know what most people think when they look at girls like me, girls who grow up without their fathers. They think we are missing a vital component of a healthy family—the loving and caring male role model who showers us with compliments, wisdom, and advice. People think girls who grow up without their fathers must feel unwanted, rejected, and abandoned. While I know some girls might feel this way, that is not my story. I don't care about my father's absence. The only problem is that my mother doesn't believe me.

My mom says it's natural for a child to want a connection with her father. She tells me that she has plenty of friends who still long for the dads who weren't present in their lives. I even found a book in her collection that explains the negative impact of growing up without a father. On the cover is a picture of a little girl waiting by a window with tears in her eyes, desperate for her father to arrive. But I've never waited desperately for my father to show up, even when he said he was going to and didn't.

My mom worries that my apathy is a façade. She thinks deep down, I'm really torn up about my father. But I believe she's been more worried about his absence than I have. I've always been fine without him, even when I was a little girl. The fact is, I have someone even better.

When I was in preschool, my best friend asked me my father's name.

"Grandpa!" I replied, without missing a beat.

My grandfather is everything a father should be and more. He's charismatic, smart, and funny and loves me more than anything in the world. He's a good listener and gives me great advice about life. He encourages me when I'm feeling down and helps me find solutions to my biggest challenges, whether they are with my friends, teachers, or even my mom. We talk on the phone almost every day, and our favorite thing to do is spend time together in dollar stores, looking for deals. He's taken me on trips to my favorite water park, too, even though he has poor eyesight and is often the oldest person there. I grew up thinking all fathers were as compassionate, attentive, and involved as my grandfather. By comparison, my own father comes up short.

From the time I was born, my father has never made it a priority to be a part of my life. He's a journalist, and when I was an infant, he moved from New York, where I live with my mother, to Africa for work. For the next several years, he would occasionally visit, sometimes with gifts. When I was a toddler, he gave me a giant stuffed bear. When I turned five, he bought me a bicycle. Then, when I was eight, he moved back to New York for good.

After all those years of rarely seeing him, my father suddenly started sending a flurry of invitations, but they were inconsistent. Every few months, he suddenly remembered I existed. Then he would send me a bunch of texts, inviting me to things I didn't want to do, like go to art museums. I knew he was trying to get to know me, but any time that we did spend together was awkward. Compared to my grandfather, I found my father cold and distant. He didn't talk much. He just stared and took pictures of me on his phone. My mother kept encouraging me to spend time with him, but I would only agree to go if I could bring my best friend, Theo. That way, I would have someone to talk to.

When I was nine, I saw my father three times: he took me to a museum, we visited an arcade, and we went out for hot chocolate. After that, I decided I didn't want to see him anymore. I didn't feel comfortable, and we never had any fun. I also didn't think it was fair that he thought he could just walk into my life whenever he felt like it. I started saying "No" to every invite, but my mother insisted I go. She warned me that if I didn't see him now, I might regret not having a relationship with him when I got older. Plus, she said I was being rude. Finally, after months of ignoring his requests, I started feeling bad. Just before I turned eleven, I decided to give my father another chance.

I agreed to meet him at a neighborhood restaurant, but only

if my mother came with me. She sat at a nearby table while he sat across from me at a table for two. Before our dinner arrived, he took out a deck of cards and laid them out on the table in a row. He flipped over the first card. On it was a picture of a blond woman, brushing her hair.

"This card represents beauty," he said.

The next card, he explained, represented good fortune. The last card he showed me had a picture of what looked like a prince with a sword.

"This represents forgiveness," he added, "and letting go of the past."

I just stared at him.

"I have a lot to offer you," he continued. "That's why I am willing to put up with your hostility."

As soon as we left the restaurant, I told my mother what happened.

"He made me feel bad," I said. "He called me *hostile,* like this is all *my* fault. I don't want to see him ever again." Then I started to cry.

"Okay," she replied with a sigh. "I won't make you."

Since then, my mother has kept her word, except on my birthday. Every year, my father texts her to say that he has a present for me, and every year, she insists that I see him. My thirteenth birthday was no different. A week before the day, he texted my mom to say that he wanted to bring me a gift.

"He said he'll be here at six o'clock," she told me. "So be ready."

Later, while I was doing my homework, I looked up and realized it was six fifteen. He was late. At six thirty, I thought there might be traffic. At seven, I started practicing piano. By nine, I began getting ready for bed. My father never showed up. I didn't really care. I certainly didn't lose any sleep over it. The next morning, I woke up bright and early and had a great day at school, just like I did all the other times he didn't show up. Afterward, he asked to meet up with me again and again, canceling at the last minute each time. I finally decided to meet my father, on *my* terms.

That is how we ended up sitting across from each other at Chipotle with an astrology book on the table between us. It was only after I left the restaurant that I opened the book and found the gift receipt stuck between the pages. The present he'd been telling my mom and me about, the one he said he'd bought a month before, was actually purchased that afternoon.

As I walked home, I thought about how my mother would make me write a thank-you note. Next year, she would make me see my father again, when he contacted her to give me another birthday present. Instead of agreeing to her terms, I decided I was going to tell my mom that I wasn't going to write my father a note for a gift that he'd put no thought into. I was also going to tell her that I didn't want see him again, not even on my birthday. I don't have to be a "good" daughter to my father because he has never been a "good" father to me.

Good fathers are there for their children. They are supportive and engaged, and they know their kids' interests and do their best to accommodate them. Good fathers care about their kids' feelings, and most important, they don't walk in and out of their children's lives at will. That is the kind of father I deserve.

Having a good father would be nice, but I'm happy with my life. I have a loving family who supports me in everything I do, and I'm working hard to achieve my dreams, with or without a father. I'm special, and I don't need anyone's attention—not even my father's—to prove it.

Now, I just have to find a way to convince my mom that I am perfectly content. ■

Who Is My Father?

DEMETREA HARDIMAN, AS TOLD TO THE EDITOR

I AM MY MOTHER'S MIDDLE CHILD. My sister, Rene, who is seven years younger, didn't grow up with her father, but she knew that he existed. She'd seen pictures of him and there was definitely some resemblance. My brother, Tre, is a year and a half older than me, and we believed that Sam, my mother's high school sweetheart, was our father. That's the story we were told, anyway.

We share a last name, and aside from the fact that he's almost a foot taller than me, Tre and I favor each other, too. Actually, we all look a lot like my mother, who looks like *her* mother. From my grandmother, whom I always called My Ol' Lady, I inherited my build and my green eyes. There is no denying that we are all family.

My brother and I went to the same junior high, and one day, a man came up to school and said that he was Tre's father. We were both kind of confused, but didn't give it too much thought, especially after the principal sent the man away because he wasn't listed on our records. But when we got home, there he was again, sitting in the living room, talking to my mother. We'd barely stepped foot into the room when she dropped the bomb.

"This is your father," she said, addressing Tre.

She didn't even look at me.

I just stood there, planted in the same spot, for what seemed like an eternity, but it probably only took a few seconds for the initial shock to wear off. The next thing I remember was going outside to hang with my friends.

Right away, the question started forming in my mind. Although I couldn't imagine what the answer could be, I thought about how the pieces of my story weren't connecting. I wondered if Tre's father might be my father, too, but that didn't seem to make sense. After all, my mother hadn't even glanced in my direction when she made their introduction. It was on that day that I asked myself, for the first time, *Who is my father?* I was twelve years old.

I believed that the man whose name was listed on my birth certificate, Sam, was my father. I had no reason to think otherwise, except for the way he treated me. Whenever I saw him with his other two daughters, whom I considered my sisters, he was always loving and warm, but when I was around, he seemed so distant. He didn't show me any affection. He didn't hug me, he barely spoke to me, and as much as I'd always hoped to look up in the stands and see him cheering for me when I was playing sports, that was never the case. There were other things that seemed odd, too, like the fact that I wasn't allowed to visit him at his house and my sisters could never come to my house for a sleepover. I couldn't figure out why I never quite fit in, but when I think back, there was an incident that occurred a few weeks before Tre's father showed up that ignited my confusion.

Sam had a big extended family, most of which lived in a complex not too far from where I lived with My Ol' Lady in Los Angeles. At her house, she treated me, Tre, and Rene like her own. My mom stayed there, too—sometimes—but that's another story I'll come back to. The complex, though? That was the hub. It's where Sam's parents, siblings, nieces, and nephews all lived, but he stayed a few miles away with his wife and two daughters. Since my mother was close with his sisters, we kids spent a lot of time there, too, ripping and running and playing with our cousins. One day, I rode my bike over by myself because I'd heard that my paternal grandmother was sick. We'd always had a pleasant relationship, so my plan was to bring her flowers and see how she was feeling. She quickly let me know that she wasn't interested.

"Don't no black people have green eyes," she spat at me. "You're the devil's child and I don't want to see you at my door again!"

Then she slammed the door in my face.

I don't recall when I started crying, but I remember throwing the flowers on the ground and hopping back on my bike. I pedaled so fast to get home, and as soon as I got inside, I could feel the tears streaming down my face. When I tried to explain to My Ol' Lady what happened, she wrapped me in her arms and did her best to console me. I was so hurt by what my paternal grandmother said, mainly because I was just beginning to understand God. All I could think was, *How could I be the devil's child when I'm being raised to love God? I thought I was His child . . . does He not love me?* As far as the color of my eyes, that came from the woman who was rubbing my back and wiping away my tears. She's the one who'd always shown me love. I knew that *she* loved God, too, so I couldn't imagine how she could be the devil's child. But was *I*?

My mother was very upset when I told her the story, but even as she declared that we wouldn't be going back to the complex, I worried about not being able to see my sisters or cousins anymore. I also tried to remember all of the things My Ol' Lady told me. She said that my paternal grandmother was probably just having a bad day because she wasn't feeling well. That was possible, but because I'd gone to see her alone, I thought maybe she'd used that as an opportunity to finally say what she really felt about me. In the moment, I don't think I questioned if her son was my father. She never said that I wasn't her granddaughter, either, but when Tre's father showed up that day, I knew something was definitely wrong. Although I didn't really understand what was going on, not right away, I could sense that I'd been lied to, for years, and that Sam was not my father. To add insult to injury, that meant his two daughters weren't my sisters, my cousins weren't really my cousins, and my paternal grandmother wasn't my grandmother after all.

Sadly, for Tre, his father didn't stick around for very long. After about a year or so, he vanished without any explanation and we never saw him again. During the time that he was around, though, I remember thinking that my brother had hit the jackpot. At least he knew who his father was. He'd had the chance to be with him, too, even though it was only for a short time. I had none of that. I watched from the sidelines as they did so many of the things I'd always dreamed that we'd do with our father. They went fishing and took trips up to the mountains and to Catalina Island. I was so jealous of the time they spent together, but because they were bonding as father and son, I didn't feel I was welcome to join them.

That was a really sad time for me, but thankfully, my anger and frustration didn't affect my relationship with Tre. Instead, I started getting in fights at school and messing up in class. I just didn't know any other way to express my feelings. No matter what I did, no matter how hard I studied or how many points I scored on the field, I started to think that maybe I wasn't good enough to have a father. Maybe I wasn't pretty enough or worthy enough either. What I wanted so much was a father, *my* father, but who was he? Where was he? And who were my people?

I immediately started asking direct questions, but nobody could give me a straight answer—not my aunts (they didn't know) or My Ol' Lady (she didn't know) and *definitely* not my mother. She'd always dismiss my questioning by waving me off with her usual words—"Oh, he's your father," speaking of Sam, but I wasn't buying it anymore and she knew it. As mad as I was about all of the lying, I still wanted to know the truth about my father. I asked if there was a chance that she didn't know who he was, and as painful as it was to consider, I even asked if I was the product of rape.

Because I wanted her to be real with me, I was willing to accept whatever answer she could give, but she didn't have one. She would just shut down. It got to the point where she'd cry or stare off into the distance whenever I asked. So, over time, I just stopped asking.

My mother. Where do I begin? I will say that we are a lot closer these days, but when I was growing up, she was a rolling stone. The baby of four, she was just like her sisters, each of whom lived hard, partied even harder, and abused drugs along the way. That's just the truth. I remember there were days and months when she would just be *gone,* leaving us in the care of My Ol' Lady. When my mother *was* home, she kept men on constant rotation. She usually stayed in her bedroom, entertaining her company, which made me question why she chose to give her attention to those men over her own kids.

My grandmother used to say that my grandfather stayed busy, too. Maybe that's where my mother got it from. After I came out to my family, at thirteen—my mother says she always knew; My Ol' Lady was nothing but accepting—I would eventually do the same thing. Years later, when I was in my early twenties, my grandmother had no problem with calling me out on the number of girlfriends I had coming in and out of her house. Looking back, I guess it was like a revolving door, but at the time, I didn't think anything of it. I was just living. Until I was checked about my irresponsible behavior, I don't think I realized that I was following in my mother's footsteps. The last thing I ever wanted to do was disappoint my grandmother.

The most consistent person in my life was always My Ol' Lady, who passed in 2007. She's the one who taught me about life and talked to me honestly. She spent time with me and by watching the way she loved her family, I learned the value of being caring and compassionate. Even though I didn't have a steady male figure in my life, I always believed that a man's job was to be the protector of his family. In our house, it was my grandmother who held that position. Eventually, that role would become mine when she was no longer able. I am also that person when it comes to my relationships. She used to school me on men, too, which I always found to be pretty funny because I've never dated any.

"Men can be dogs, but there are good dogs and bad ones," she'd say. "Some can be loving and take care of you, but you have to be willing to compromise and know that if you're not tending him, another woman will. And you don't want him laying hands on you and then turning around talking about love."

I heard what My Ol' Lady said about dealing with men, but I used to wonder if my mother ever did. Of her many boyfriends, one of them stuck around longer than the rest. They dated for almost four years and during that time, he became the first man to ever treat me like a daughter. I called him "Dad." He showed me attention, spent time with me, and when I got older, we'd ride motorcycles, talk about women, and just hang out. I stayed close to him after they broke up, but as I later discovered, he was physically abusive to many of his past girlfriends, including my mother. Again, I looked at her and wondered, *Why?* Why would she allow that type of person to be around her kids and act as a father figure to me? There are some things that will never make sense.

As for Sam, I haven't talked to him in years. Tre has remained in touch with him, but I never saw the point. It's not in my nature to hold onto hard feelings, but it's also not easy to forget all of the doubt and confusion I felt whenever I was in his presence. Until this day, I don't understand the nature of the relationship he had with my mother, but as an adult, I've chosen not to subject myself to someone who doesn't care about me or my feelings.

My sister, Rene, was thirty-two years old when she finally met her father. He'd just been a man in a picture until her half sister found her on Facebook. My mother was really happy that Rene would be able to meet the other side of her family. I was happy for her, too, but I couldn't help but think about my unanswered question. I can't say that I expected my mother to have any new information to share with me about my father, but I really wish she would have said something to acknowledge the obvious—I am the only one of her three children who does not have a father. That's just what it is, I guess, and I have to make peace with it. I'm not sure I have another choice.

As I've gotten older and had my own experiences, I have a better understanding of the weight my mother must carry because of the mistakes she's made, and why reliving the past might be painful for her. I don't ask her about my father anymore, but I have come to believe that whoever he is, it's likely that he doesn't even know I exist. That makes me feel pretty fucked up, because it makes me think of how he missed out on knowing me, too.

What I'm thankful for these days is that my mother and I have gotten closer. After she was diagnosed with cancer, I stayed by her side and have cared for her every step of the way. Although she's still fighting for her life, I think My Ol' Lady would be happy to know that we are in it together. She taught me well, and I continue to live by her example.

It took a lot for me to become the person I am today, to be really comfortable in my skin and love *me*, unconditionally. Regardless of my upbringing and the experiences that I once felt I'd missed out on, I think I turned out to be a pretty decent woman. A lot of people have traveled similar roads—from growing up in the 'hood to not having a father—and they've had a much harder time coping. I am one of the strong ones who survived, and I'm proud of myself for getting to the other side, with my heart and spirit intact. ■

Again

DANIELLE RENE

I COULDN'T FACE MY MOM to tell her that I'd believed him and was now disappointed. So, I just climbed into her bed and laid my head on her lap. She knew, without me saying a word. We'd had years of experience.

He disappeared, again.

"If you let him back into your life, that is your decision, Baby Girl," she said. "Just don't get your hopes up."

It was a familiar narrative. And I defended him, every time.

"He's my father!" I'd always say, defiantly, before running off to answer his calls or trying to see him while he was in town. Then like clockwork, in a few days or months, I'd be climbing back into her bed to lay my head on her lap, again.

When I was in elementary school, I remember having a conversation with my dad, which ended with his promise to call me for my birthday and send a present. My mother quickly took the phone and the same argument ensued.

"You're not the one who has to pick up the broken pieces," she yelled. "Stop promising her things and not delivering!"

I remember hating her for that. I thought, *He doesn't deliver because you always argue with him,* but I wasn't brave enough to say that out loud. Instead, I just went to my room and cried. And I waited. After my birthday came, and went, I climbed into her bed and asked her how he could forget about me.

He'd disappointed me, again.

That's what our relationship has always been, my father and me—an emotional roller coaster of irregular guest appearances. But still, I did not give up on him. Every year, I would ask my mother if I could send him a Fathers Day card, and every year, I would painstakingly pick out the perfect one. I didn't know anything about him, not even his birthday, so sending a card on Fathers Day was the best I could do. She would watch me and just shake her head, but I'd always say, "He's my father."

Those three words—*he's my father*—became my defense each and every time I tried to establish a relationship with him. Maybe I hoped that saying those words over and over would somehow make them true. Even though I didn't know what having a father actually meant, I still wanted to have one—*mine*—anyway.

My mother and father met while he was still with another woman—the mother of my half brother and sister. After his relationship with my mom ended, he went back to his family. That's the only story I know. I was too young to remember him ever holding me or seeing the two of them hold each other.

Long before I was born, my parents' families were intertwined through marriages and long-term friendships. His sister married my mom's brother. His cousin married my mom's other brother. A host of cousins grew up together in our hometown, but I never really got to know them. My grandfather, my mom's father, lived in the same house for forty years, and I spent many summers there, which was a well-known fact to everyone. If he wanted to, my father could always find me, and when he *did* want to, I usually ended up feeling like an outsider whenever I spent time with him and his family.

"He has *another* daughter?" one of my paternal cousins would whisper just within earshot. They hoped I didn't hear them, but I always did.

"Yes, he has *three* children—two daughters and a son," another cousin would reply, then shuffle me over to be examined and hugged. I was extremely jealous that my half siblings not only knew what it felt like to live in a house with my dad, but they knew his family, too. They also shared inside jokes with him and group photos. I would watch them interact with each other and think, *He really loves them. He knows them. He just thinks he should love me, but does he?*

I would avoid thinking about the whispers I overheard about me and my mother—and my dad's "habits." His first love was drugs. His second love was crime. Perhaps there just wasn't much room in his life to love all of his children because he spent so much time chasing a high. My father never used drugs in front of me, but I felt the consequences of his secrets. I felt his absences. Sometimes I wondered when my mother knew. Did she think she could save him? If so, I've inherited that same insane way of loving someone, and have often drowned in the process of thinking I could be a life raft.

"I'm clean now," he said during one of our conversations. He even worked hard to become a drug counselor. That might sound like the blind leading the blind, but apparently he was pretty good at it. He'd always been good at playing the role, even when he couldn't stay committed to it for very long. Then a few months later, the whispers started again. Jail time. Drug charges. And there I was, again, without a father.

My father once called to apologize to me. By that time, I was in high school, and he'd just been released from yet another stint in jail.

"I got your Fathers Day card and I was so happy," he said. "I'm sorry that I was never there, but I knew you didn't need me."

It felt like the earth stopped spinning for a minute.

"I knew you'd be okay because you have a good mom," he said. "People told me that my family and my kids hated me, but when I got your card, I knew they were wrong."

I broke down crying. I thought that finally, *finally*, he understood. All of my attempts to love him, despite his distance—and all of those Fathers Day cards—were paying off. But it wasn't long before I ended up laying my head on my mother's lap.

He disappeared, again.

When I matured to the age when romantic love becomes a priority, I didn't realize that I'd already been set up for failure. Despite having a wonderful grandfather and uncles—my mom's brothers—who stepped in as my father figures, I didn't lean into their examples. Instead, I looked to my father.

My relationship with my father taught me that no matter how much unconditional love you give to someone, getting love in return was not a guarantee. It was just an option. So, I found men who were distant charmers and loved me just as he did—selfishly. Again and again, I attached myself to the smallest hint of affection, afraid of being left behind. I would peacock around to get noticed and be loved, and then I would tolerate men who dropped in and out of my life whenever it was convenient for them. I fell for men who were still in love with ghosts of girlfriends past or just in love with themselves and "not ready" to be with me. In the meantime, they didn't mind enjoying my company, my body, my money, and my affection, of course. The kind of hurt I felt when they left was so familiar to me. I knew what it was, and I clung to it. I thought I had to *give* for them to want to be—and stay—with me. It would take years of prayer and many hours of therapy to bring the real issue to light, but the damage was already done.

By the time I was eighteen, whenever my father would make an appearance, I was too bitter and exhausted from my own relationships to try anymore. I took it out on him. I wanted him to hurt. I was dull and short on the phone. I rarely returned calls. I even stopped sending Fathers Day cards. I kept the details of my life private and pushed him away anytime he tried to get close to me. *Oh, he'll just stop calling in a month anyway,* I thought. *Why bother?*

He would always prove me right.

"You act like you don't want to hear from me," he said one day. I had nothing to say in response. I just wanted him to go away. And he did. For all the years I tried so hard to love him, I realized that he wasn't much of a fighter. One too many cold shoulders and he retreated to his usual place on the outskirts of my life. Sometimes I'd get updates from family members, but for most of my teenage years and twenties, it was pretty much radio silence.

One day, I logged into Facebook and saw that my dad had sent me a "friend" request. I stared at the computer screen, thinking it was a joke. But it wasn't. There he was, in a grainy photo. I noticed that my half siblings were mutual friends of ours, so yes, it was really him. I knew he was alive because my half brother and sister would post photos from birthday parties and family reunions. In a way, not much had changed since I was a little girl watching his family joke and laugh with each other. I had a front-row view of my dad's life, without me in it. I felt numb to it. And now he wanted to be my "friend"?

I poured myself a glass of wine and sank into a place where I hadn't been in a while—wondering about my father. *Should I do this to myself again? Should I try again?* Yes, but cautiously. I accepted his request, and he quickly started commenting on all of my status updates and photos. I had to laugh because I now had the same complaints as my other friends: "Oh my gosh, my dad is such a bad Facebooker. He comments on *everything!*" I can admit that I was kind of proud to have a "dad" story. It was also from Facebook that I finally learned his birthday.

We eventually started communicating regularly through Messenger. I was surprised that I didn't cringe when I typed, "Hi, Dad." I knew there was no way to make up for the lost time, so I tried to put my bitterness to the side, for my own sanity. I would allow him a peek into my internet life, and maybe I would learn more about him along the way. He told me about his new job, his new life, and how he had it all together again. It was the same old story, but I believed him. I *needed* to believe him as much as I needed to forgive him, so I could move past the hurt I felt for myself. I drew boundaries around the details I shared with him and made sure to engage him only to a point. I didn't want to inflict any more stress or hurt upon myself. I was hoping for the best, but I braced myself, just in case.

A few weeks after we became "friends," I noticed that he hadn't answered my last message. He stopped updating his profile, too, and he no longer commented on my status updates. Then I got a message from his girlfriend, who happened to be the same age as me. "Have you seen your dad?" she asked. "I can't reach him."

Before I responded, I sent a message to my half sister to ask if something was going on. "He's back in the streets again," she wrote back. "Ignore his girlfriend."

Yes, he'd disappeared, again.

This time, I didn't lay my head on my mother's lap. There was no need. He was being the man I'd always known, doing what he'd always done. But unlike in the past, my heart wasn't broken. Not again. I had finally realized that my dad is, like all of us, human. He's just a man, battling an addiction and years of his own hurt and bullshit. I now understand that his absences were likely an act of grace. Perhaps God spared me from the dark side of his life, the one that my half siblings had to endure.

I have learned how to love others despite their humanness. I know what it means to extend grace and mercy to others, while keeping boundaries so I can still love myself in the process. I have learned to forgive, and I've come to a place of understanding what love is by *not* accepting what it isn't. I've also stopped using my father's shortcomings as a reflection of my worth.

All that said, I have tried to be prepared for the day when he comes back. Some days, I think about writing him just to let it all out and ask why he never loved me, consistently, as a father should. The crumbs that he left for me were always enough to keep me wanting more, but I was severely malnourished at the same time. I want to ask him if he remembers the day we danced at a wedding, or if he even remembers my birthday. I also want to yell at him for not warning me about the men in the world who are just like him.

Most of the time, I find that I'm bracing myself for the day I have to bury him. That would be his final disappearance and the end of any chance of us ever having a relationship. I can admit that I would miss him because he's my father, even though I still don't know what that really means. ∎

A Lesson from My Mother

NICOLE SHEALEY

My CHILDHOOD WOULD HAVE BEEN unstable whether my father was around or not. Since he wasn't there, I can't speak to what that experience might have been. I can only tell the story of my life as it was—and it was a mess.

I grew up a child in flux. On weekdays, my younger sister and I were shuttled between home, school, and our grandmother's house, which were all within a fifteen-mile radius of each other in Massachusetts. My mother used Granny's address in Roxbury so we could attend an elementary school in her district. I can imagine that it wasn't safe for two young girls to be latchkey kids, so my mother drove us to school, and later, we'd walk to Granny's house with our cousins and the other kids from the neighborhood. When my mother was done with work, she'd pick me and my sister up, and the three of us would head home for the night. That was the routine, on a good day.

But about my father . . .

I remember seeing a few pictures of me with my father, but because he left when I was four years old, I don't have any memories of him. I suppose I never found it odd that he wasn't in my life because there weren't many fathers around when I was growing up. I don't recall seeing any fathers drop off or pick up their kids from school, attend Christmas plays, or participate in back-to-school nights. A small handful of my friends had fathers at home, but the majority did not. All of the single mothers I knew were struggling—including mine—so I believed that kids who lived with their fathers were wealthy. I had no idea what it meant to have two parents at home. That wasn't my reality. Some say that a father is the man by whom a girl measures all men, but because my father wasn't around, there was so much I didn't know. Ironically, a lot of what I learned about men came from watching my mother.

She was once a secretary at a local university, but within a short time, she was promoted to work directly with one of the deans. It was a good job, and I'm sure that from the outside looking in, my mother appeared to have it all together. In reality, she was nowhere near together—as a woman or a mother. I never understood what she might have been missing in her life, but back when she was young and beautiful, she was rarely without a man on her arm. She always seemed to *need* to be with a man, just because. Whenever my sister and I were out with her—whether running errands or just walking down the street—it was hard not to notice the attention she received from men. It was almost as if we weren't there. I think it's something that we got used to, just like we got used to the amount of company she kept.

My mother dated. A lot. There were always men in and out of our house, and I never felt safe. When she had date nights during the week, she would leave us with Granny after school. If her dates went especially well, she'd drop off our school clothes for the next day. Most nights, I wasn't sure where I would be laying my head, but I always looked forward to being at Granny's house. When we stayed there, I knew I'd get a good night's sleep and not be on edge about an altercation that might pop off in the next room. At Granny's, we had clean clothes, and because she dried her linen outside on a clothesline, the sheets smelled like sunshine. I remember, too, that we'd wake up to a home-cooked breakfast before heading off to school. Being at her house was the closest that my life came to being normal.

Another reason why I loved being at Granny's was because she lived in a "family home." That meant we were surrounded by generations of love. On each of the three floors there was someone who was related to me, all on my mother's side. My great-aunt lived in the first floor apartment with her family, my grandmother had the second floor, and my great-grandmother lived on the third floor. Because we had the whole house, my sister and I got to hang out with our cousins, of every age, who were always around. We had time to play, do our homework, and eat dinner, but as soon as my mother drove up, the party was over.

While Granny wasn't aware that my mother sometimes allowed men to sleep over when my sister and I were there, she knew things weren't right, and that we had no structure at home. She was very concerned about what was going on at our house and often spoke to my mother about how she was living. I remember trying my best to eavesdrop on their hushed, heated conversations, but my grandmother was careful not to allow things to go too far. After all, we were her grandchildren, not her *children*, and I suppose she didn't want to poke the bear too hard. I think she was unsure about what my mother might do—or what she was capable of doing—when it came to balancing her social life with parenting.

Many of my mother's boyfriends were problematic, which is something else I don't think Granny knew. Some were lazy. Some were drug addicts. Some were mean. Some were territorial. Some were dumb. Some were sneaks. The worst of them were physically abusive—but instead of leaving these relationships, my mother tolerated bad behavior for far too long. She covered bruises with makeup or a swoop of hair over her eye and kept ice handy to ease the swelling of any welts on her body. When she was unable to hide her injuries, she'd call in sick, which meant that my sister and I didn't make it to school. We missed a lot of school. Having a man in our house always meant uncertainty. I'd wonder if the cops would be called or if my sister and I would be whisked away to Granny's house in the middle of the night. Anything was possible, but after a while I just stopped caring because I knew that no matter how badly any man treated my mother, she'd forgive him and take him back. She always took them back—except for two.

When I was in first grade, my mother married a man who was a drug addict. For the four years they were together, he lived between our apartment and a rehab center, where she'd force me and my sister to visit him on "Family Day." When he stayed with us, he'd often disappear for days at a time. He also stole from us to feed his habit. Sometimes it was money, or even the television, that would go missing, and there were times when my sister and I couldn't find our good toys. There was physical abuse going on, too, and my mother was often as guilty as he was when it came to slapping and hitting. None of that was enough for her to break it off with him, though. Then after one of their big arguments, we left him in the apartment and fled to Granny's house until things cooled down a bit. When we returned later that night, I was relieved to see that he was gone and hadn't stolen anything else. Everything seemed to be in its place.

My sister and I were hungry before we went to bed that night, so my mother said we could each have a bowl of cereal. As we were eating, my sister looked at me and said that her cereal tasted funny. Mine did, too. I screamed for my mother and when I told her that something was wrong with the cereal, she started sifting through the box. Then she sniffed the box.

"Get your coats," she said, frantically. "We have to get to the emergency room."

We spent several hours at Boston Children's Hospital, and I'll never forget the terror I felt when the nurse tried to keep me calm as she explained how she was going to put a tube up my nose, down my throat, and into my stomach. My mother's husband had sprayed insect repellent into our cereal box, and both my sister and I had to have our stomachs pumped. That incident would finally put an end to my mother's relationship with him, but only after the cops were called a few times because he'd broken into our apartment after she changed the locks. Then we moved.

As if being poisoned by my mother's husband wasn't traumatic enough, the man who stands out the most is the one who sent our already erratic home life into a complete tailspin. When I was ten years old, my mother, with the help of our uncle, packed up our house, dropped us off at Granny's, and moved to Texas, where our family roots run deep. Her move was abrupt, and it wasn't for a good reason. She didn't leave us to pursue a better job or to further her education. Instead, she moved to get away from a man who was not only physically and emotionally abusive, but also mentally unbalanced. He stalked her, beat her, and once even attempted to abduct her in broad daylight. Remembering the trauma he inflicted on me and my sister still makes me sick to my stomach.

One night, he grabbed our cat and a brown paper bag and went out to the back porch. I never saw that cat again, and my mother insisted that we never speak of the incident. But the most horrifying event occurred when this man killed our parakeets, which we'd named Winston and Salem after the brands of cigarettes my mother smoked. One day, without warning, he barged into the living room, knife in hand, and killed our birds through their cage, right in front of us. I was so terrified that I just stood there and peed on myself.

My sister and I lived with our grandmother for more than a decade. Life at her house was stable and drama free, but as soon as my mother left, the questions began. Not having a father wasn't that unusual, but if your mother was gone, too, you were the odd man out. What kind of a mother just leaves her kids? And how do you explain where she is, why she left, and when she's coming back? I started making up stories just to keep people off my back. My most elaborate story was that my parents were in Texas, together, and would be sending for us as soon as they saved up enough money. I was always imagining something else, another scenario, that would make sense to other people and to me.

While I was weaving intricate tales to my friends, my mother had started a new life in Texas with a man who was not my father. During one of my visits, she introduced me to her new boyfriend, who was well-educated, drove fine cars, and wore tailored suits. He seemed to treat her well, until I learned the truth during a conversation that I wasn't supposed to hear: he was married. After the drama I'd witnessed when I lived with her as a child, I can't say that I was surprised. My mother is who she is, always has been.

I was nineteen when she returned to Boston. She lived with us at Granny's for a few difficult, stressful months before she left to be with yet another man. This time, she opted for a man from the neighborhood, someone we all knew. In record time, she moved in with him, got married (and still is), and gave birth to my baby brother.

Having watched so many of her relationships crash and burn was exhausting, to say the least, but I never thought about what life might have been like if my father was there. The truth is, when your father isn't in your life, he's simply a stranger. I didn't have daydreams about him drifting in to save the day or sort through our messiness. My mother never spoke of my father, and if I picked up the phone today and asked her about him, she'd be silent and then get upset with me. She does not, will not, and cannot speak to me in a mature manner about him. Growing up, I asked a few of my mother's relatives about him, and they'd share a few tidbits about what he looked like or his personality. If I said or did something a certain way, Granny would comment that I looked like my father, or his sisters, but that's about it. For the most part, everyone was silent about him, and eventually, I became silent, too. To me, he was an enigma, not a real person. There was a time, during my teenage years, when I preoccupied myself with wondering if I might have other siblings. My biggest fear was that one day I'd meet Mr. Right, only to discover that he was my half brother. Just the thought of that scared the hell out of me.

After everything I'd seen growing up, I knew I didn't want to get tangled in an abusive relationship or be with somebody who didn't want to be with me. At a very young age, I'd made peace with the idea that I could live the rest of my life as a single, child-less woman. I lived by that principal until the day the man I would later marry walked into the retail store where I worked during col-lege. When we met, I wasn't looking for a boyfriend and definitely wasn't thinking about a husband. I remember that he was outgoing and funny, but because he was from New York, I didn't think our friendship would go much further than long-distance phone calls. But my feelings eventually changed. I noticed that whenever he was in town, he showed up when he said he would and did what he said he'd do. He treated me well, he treated his friends well, and although his family—led by a strong-willed single mother—was dramatic in its own way, I noticed that he was always the voice of reason. He was solid, and because I'd never encountered a man like him, I gave him a chance. Neither one of us came from much, and we definitely didn't grow up with positive role models, but I think of us as a pair of sunflowers that bloomed despite the odds.

The issue of my father's absence arose when my husband and I started our family. During each of my pregnancies, my amnio-centesis tests came back abnormal, which was really scary. That's when it hit home for me that I had no information about my fa-ther or his family's medical history. My husband's parents weren't together, but he had a great relationship with his father and could pick up the phone and ask questions. I wasn't able to do that, which was hurtful and frustrating. Thankfully, both of our boys were born healthy, but at the time, the not-knowing was overwhelming, espe-cially because it could have affected my children.

Might my life have been different if my father was around? I can't say, but I'll never know. I don't really think about it much. For all I know, he could be alive or dead. He could be successful or living on the streets. I don't have a clue about what his life is or was, but I do know he was aware that he had two little girls out in the world that he left behind. He didn't care if we had enough to eat or if there was enough money to make rent. He didn't worry about our safety, nor did he concern himself with the men who came in and out of our lives when we lived with our mother. I'll never know the reasons why he left me and my sister, or why he never bothered to connect with us. He simply erased us from his life, and I have accepted that.

My sons are teenagers now, and soon they'll be leaving the nest. As they mature into young men, I see pieces of me and my husband in both of them. They are the sum of our best parts. In my husband, I see a man who kept his promises to me, to himself, and to our children. He's the type of father I wish we'd both had, but it's impossible to rewrite the past. We can only look toward the future, which is what I've chosen to do.

Knowing that my children have grown up in a stable household has been the truest blessing. They have never lived in fear, as I once did, and they've always known that their parents are present, loving, and supportive. Thankfully, my Granny lived long enough to witness me became a woman, a wife, and a mother. It wasn't easy to get to this place, but I know she would be so proud of me. ■

My Sugar Pie

DESNEY BUTLER, AS TOLD TO THE EDITOR

AT SEVENTY-THREE YEARS OLD, I've got a lot to say about this life I've lived. Having come from a poor family, I grew up as the youngest of three in a single-parent household. My mother told me that I used to say I wanted five sons, but not a husband. Why I hoped for all boys, I don't know, but perhaps I was ambivalent about marriage because I didn't have a father figure at home. I remember that my father tried to spend time with me and provided my mother with financial help on occasion, but I always wanted him to be *present*. That wish didn't come true for me until he could no longer care for himself.

In my family, we greet one another with a kiss on the mouth. When I think of my father, I can still remember the feel of his lips because they were so firm. As a little girl, he seemed to tower over me, over the *world*, like he was seven feet tall. He was a healthy man—not fat, just nice and healthy—and he had this scent about him. They say that a girl's father is the first man she loves, and the father I *thought* I had was whom I adored. He called me Sugar Pie, and I called him Sugar Pie, too.

My parents were never married. My mother was single and worked as a domestic, but I know she wanted more for herself and her children. Although my older brother and sister shared the same father, I was my mother and father's only child together. I was always very close to my siblings, but my mother once said that my father wasn't very nice to them, nor did he want to take care of a woman with two other children, which is why she left him when I was a toddler. My father, who was fifteen years older than my mother, also had a son, but he died before I was born.

My earliest memory of my father dates back to when I was about eight years old. He came to Brooklyn to pick me up and we drove out to Long Branch, New Jersey, where I spent the summer with him and one of my aunts. Because he didn't come around too often, I remember being overjoyed just knowing that this man, driving this grand car, was *my* father. He was into politics then and worked closely with Thomas E. Dewey, who eventually became the governor of New York. Sometimes his image would flash across those newsreels that ran before movies, and I'd point at the screen and scream, "That's my father, *that's* my father!" but my friends always laughed at me. These many years later, I can understand why they didn't believe that the man up on the big screen could possibly be my father—they'd never seen him.

Eventually, my father stopped taking me for the summers, and the only time we saw each other was when I went to *him*. By the time I was twelve and old enough to take the subway by myself, I'd ride up to Harlem, where he had a room at his cousin's house. I remember thinking I was so grown, traveling all the way uptown to pick up an envelope for my mother, but I never dared a peek to see how much money was inside. Sometimes, I'd even spend the weekend with him and when I awoke, in his big bed, I'd look over and watch him sleeping soundly in the chair next to me. Those silent moments were just so wonderful. Now, I don't remember what we talked about or even what we did together during those visits, but I was so happy to be with him.

When I was growing up, our house was often filled with extended family, but there wasn't a man in my household. My brother was there, of course, but he was eight years older than me and trying to find his way in the world. On the rare occasion when my father came by our house, he'd kiss my mother on her cheek and put his arms around her, which seemed so sweet when I was a child. But as I got older and began to learn more about life, I was annoyed by the fact that she only showed her femininity when a man was around. I also remember one of her boyfriends, whom she called Honey. She always seemed to be a different person in his presence, which I didn't like, nor did I like the fact that he was a married man. I hated watching her sit around waiting for him and being second. That's when I began to envy my girlfriends who had their fathers around, full time. Although I later learned that their families were not as happy as I'd imagined them to be, all I saw were the good times they shared with their fathers, and I wanted what I believed they had.

My mother used to say that I got my personality from my father. I was always a fighter. I'd fight on the way home from school and curse at the drop of a hat. My mother never raised her voice. She was a mild-mannered woman, but she was very strict. She didn't allow me to go to parties or have boyfriends, and I remember when she put an end to my trips to Harlem because I'd lied about going to visit my father. Instead, I went to see a boy I liked. Let's just say that I got so caught up in what I was doing that I never made it to my father's house. It's been so long that I don't remember how she found out where I was, but I'll never forget that she came and got me. That was the last time I was allowed to go uptown by myself.

Being a foolish young girl, I eventually made my own mistakes. I was a latchkey kid before that term was popular, and I recall being quite lonely as an adolescent. I started my life early, and when I got pregnant at sixteen, I was fearless—*after* I told my mother, of course. At the time, my friends said things like, "Girl, I would have never had a baby. I'd rather have gotten an abortion than tell my mother because my family would kill me," but I don't remember my pregnancy being much of an issue for my mother. Needless to say, I was busy, and by the time I turned eighteen, I'd given birth to two sons—with different fathers—and still lived under her roof.

Because my girlfriends stayed in school, attended proms, and did all of the things that teenagers do, I soon became an outcast. I also found myself constantly fighting for respect because after you've had a child young, *and* not been married, you become a different kind of girl. You're an easy mark. Many of the boys in my neighborhood who'd once thought of me as a little sister now saw me as a woman to be used, and I wasn't going for it. I knew I'd messed up, though. I was an unwed teenage mother and I hadn't finished school. And even though I was completely dependent on my mother and sister, who took care of everything, I remember feeling good just knowing that these babies were *mine.*

I was not in contact with my father during my early years of motherhood. He didn't tell me directly, but I knew he was aware that I'd had two children, and he wasn't very happy about it. I don't recall all of the feelings I was experiencing during that time of my life, but I have to wonder if his absence contributed to me making bad choices. Perhaps I would have taken another path if I'd known that I had more choices, but there was no one in my life to give me direction or say, "I want you to go to school."

On one particular night, after my sister and I moved into our own place with our children, I decided to go out with a few friends. My sister was planning a night out with her friends, too, but when they rang the bell, they were with a guy, Ben, who I remembered meeting the night before. While my sister's friends were hanging out in the front of the apartment, I was in the back pressing my hair, and my niece was keeping her eye on my boys. Ben must have caught a glimpse of my youngest son in the baby changer because he called the house the next day and asked me how my little boy was doing. Then it was my turn to ask the questions.

"Which one?" I asked.

There was a brief silence, then he shot back, "Well, how many do you *have*?"

"I have two. My other son is a year and a half and the baby is two months."

Then, without pause, he said, "Oh, what the hell."

It was on from there.

At twenty-two, Ben was four years older than me, was raised by both his mother and father, and represented everything I never had at home. He came from a good family that owned a local business. Needless to say, I was *impressed*. He had his own car, which was unusual for a young black man during that time, and every day before work, he'd take me and the boys to the park, where we'd sit by the lake and feed the ducks. Because I was accustomed to trolley cars and transit trains, I rarely ventured too far from my neighborhood, but he'd take me on dates to the delicatessen, and we'd talk and order meatballs. I was grateful to meet somebody who wasn't bothered by the fact that I had two children and wasn't interested in going to bed with me, at first. Years later, he told me that that's what he'd wanted, but he was just too scared to say anything. I'm glad he kept that to himself because I would have certainly chased him away.

The 1950s were just beginning, and it was completely unheard of for an unmarried couple to live together—let alone have children out of wedlock—but that's what Ben and I did. Again, I was busy and soon had another baby—my third son with a third man. I had no question in my mind about having a baby for a man who was taking care of me and my two young children. I loved him and would have married him even if I didn't like him, but there was no talk of marriage for the first eight years we lived together. We only decided to make it official when it was time to send the kids to Catholic school.

After a few years of being out of touch with my father, I went up to Harlem to visit him with Ben and our three boys. At the time, he didn't know that we weren't married yet, but I wanted him to know that I had gotten it together. I was almost rubbing it in his face, like, *See!* Both Ben and my father were Republicans, and they talked and talked about politics. As I sat back and watched the two of them, I wasn't completely sure what my father was thinking about me having three kids, but I could see he was happy that at least I had a man with me. I was happy about having a man with me, too, but I was also starting to learn that being in a relationship required some adjustment.

Prior to meeting Ben, my mother and sister were my dominant caregivers, but when he and I got together, he had to have complete control, which caused a great deal of tension. I had sense enough to know that he was offering me a future and people respected me for who *he* was, but I also knew the situation, and our relationship wasn't perfect. We fought constantly and there was a lot of on-and-off and back-and-forth in the relationship. He used to jokingly say that he thought his middle name was "Motherfucker" because I called him one so often. I don't think we started to get it together until I'd given birth to my fourth son when I was twenty.

My mother used to take care of children, so my instinct for caring for my sons came from her. Learning how to be a wife, however, took years and years. I knew what I wanted for my family, so I tried to keep in step with my roles as a wife and stay-at-home mother, but I was only willing to take so much nonsense from my husband. As much as my family liked Ben for the life he provided for me and the kids, they didn't like seeing what they thought I had to take to have it. But I knew that life didn't work that way. It's about give and take. Although the fighting continued for a while, we slowly learned and grew to respect each other. It took some time for us to get it together, though.

When I was twenty-nine and pregnant with my fifth son, my father got very ill and lost all of his money. He was accused of jamming ballot boxes, and although he didn't go to jail, most of his political ties were severed. Whatever money he'd made during his career must have been hanging in his closet, because he was always sharp, but he never owned any property or had his own apartment. Over time, I noticed that he seemed to move from place to place and was always living with a different woman. I remember calling him at one woman's house, and he sounded so weak. My family had moved to Queens by that time, so I said to him, "You get in a cab and come to me." That was the summer of 1960.

Along with having a family of my own, I was also taking care of my father, who never got well again. He was undernourished, so I fed him. I'd become accustomed to fixing big, family-style meals, but my father loved simple, one-pot meals like hoppin' john. Beans, rice, and pigtails were good enough for him. Because he hadn't been able to take care of himself, he was very dirty, so I bathed him. He also had a boil on his back that needed attention, but because he was a Harlem resident, I couldn't take him to a clinic in Queens. I didn't know what to do, and other than sleeping on our sunporch, on a pull-out couch, he had nowhere to go.

It was very stressful to watch as my father withered away, but I didn't get much support from my husband. He felt it was unfair that I had to be the one to take care of someone who, for so many years, had not been a father to me. Because he was *my* father, and I was his only living child, I felt responsible for him. He had two sisters, including my aunt whom I'd visited during the summers all those years ago, and I resented them because they were only around when he was doing well financially. Some people hold grudges and are angry about things from the past, but I never felt that way about my father. I had no regrets about taking him in.

I cried a lot during that time and often called my mother in tears. She always lent me her ear and constantly prodded me to ask my father what I should do if "something happened." I was afraid to have that conversation with him, but I eventually got my nerve up to discuss his arrangements. That's when he told me to call the Masons, who would take care of everything. As relieved and satisfied as I was to have an answer, I was also saddened because his health continued to decline. Then one day, I asked a neighbor to give us a ride to a hospital in Harlem, where he was checked in almost immediately. I sat with him for a while, and we both laughed when he pointed to one of the nurses and said, "If I was younger, I would be chasing her around this bed." I remember that conversation like it was yesterday because it was the first time I really saw him as, simply, a *man*.

My father died when I was in my early thirties, but I never knew exactly when or how. I recall that he'd checked himself out of the hospital and moved in with one of his sisters, but I had less and less contact with him. I didn't have much of a relationship with my aunt either, so she didn't keep me informed about his health, nor did she feel obliged to get him to the phone when I called.

I'll forever be haunted by the fact that I was unable to attend his funeral. I was caught up with taking care of my own family, and unfortunately, my husband was not very cooperative where my paternal family was concerned. Although my father had told me that the Masons would make sure I received his insurance once he passed, I guess I was too embarrassed to ask, "Is this for me?" My mother wanted me to find out if I'd been left anything, but it turned out that he'd left the money to his sister. I had a husband who was taking care of me, so I didn't really want for anything, but my mother felt it was owed to me. I didn't feel that way.

After my father's death, I eventually lost my mother to cancer. Later, both my brother and sister died, too. Those losses were devastating, but because we were a close-knit family, we'd spent a lot of time together and in the end, there was closure. I can't say the same about my father. Until this day, I still don't feel as though we had a proper goodbye, and I'm unable to visit his grave because I don't know where he's buried. I don't even know if he has a gravestone.

And since I didn't have a relationship with his family aside from his two sisters, I wouldn't even know where to begin unraveling his history. Those things are important to know, just for your own peace of mind. He's been gone more than forty years, and I'm left with so many unanswered questions, which makes me feel quite melancholy at times.

Today, I have been a widow for almost twenty-five years, and I am a grandmother of thirteen and a great-grandmother of thirteen. Beginning with my five sons, whom I once dreamed of having, and all of the kids I've cared for over the years, I've been surrounded by children since I was sixteen years old. Because I've run a daycare center and have watched more children grow up than I can count, I believe I can determine, on sight, if a young girl or boy is being raised by a single parent. Although most women do better than men at raising children on their own, it's important for children to see their parents working *together*, even if they're not married. I like what I see in a child when both of their parents are present in their lives. Children deserve to be surrounded by love, fun, and laughter. They should also see their parents hug and kiss.

I have lived a long life full of joy and struggle, laughter and tears. When I look back, I have few regrets. I love my family and although I wish the circumstances could have been different, I would have had the same children. But I also would have completed my education. I didn't master the book smarts, but I'm thankful to God for giving me the strength to make it through. ■

Here and There

SIMONE I. SMITH, AS TOLD TO THE EDITOR

M Y MOTHER USED TO CALL HIM "STUPID."
Whenever he called the house to speak to me, she'd say, "Simone, come here . . . *Stupid's* on the phone."

It didn't matter what she said; I was always happy to talk to him. I believed him every time he promised to come see me, too. Sometimes he showed up and we'd have such a good time together. Then there were those times when I'd sit on the stoop for hours, waiting for him to walk down the block. That's when she got loud.

"I told you Stupid was *not* coming," she'd yell from inside. "He's so full of shit and I don't know why you're out there wasting your time!"

That was all such a long time ago, and thankfully, I can laugh about it now. My mother was something else. That was just her way, and because I was mouth almighty and always so sassy, I didn't think twice about speaking up.

"Stop saying that," I'd yell back. "My daddy is *not* stupid!"

I loved my father and you couldn't tell me *nothing* about him, especially when I was a little girl. But as I got older, I could see that he had problems. He was there and *not* there, and truthfully, he was never much of a parent to me or any of his other children, including three of my four brothers. It took a long time for me to figure that out because I always had a wonderful man in my life.

When I think about the true meaning of a father, the first person who comes to mind is George Samuel Pyle, Jr. He was my grand-father, my mother's father. He was the man who raised me as well as my youngest brother, who was born when I was eleven and had a different father. Papa was a God-fearing, hardworking family man and he just adored my grandmother, Oma. He worked for an air-line for more than twenty-five years, then as a handyman, and even though he never made much more than $15,000 a year, Papa was a great provider. He and Oma bought our house on 198th Street in St. Albans, Queens, when my mother and uncle were just kids, and he retired, at eighty-four, after making the last mortgage payment, because he wanted to leave something for his grandchildren. That's the type of man Papa was. He set the standard.

Most of my childhood memories are centered around my grandparent's house, but I do have one memory of the short time I lived with my parents. We were staying in the downstairs apart-ment of a two-family house off of Linden Boulevard and my bed-room was up front, by the window. One night, my mother came home and couldn't find my father. She was walking up and down the hallway calling out his name. When she finally found him, he was laying on the floor with what looked like blood all over him. She couldn't tell that it was ketchup, at first, but when she got closer to him, he busted out laughing. He was always a jokester, and although my mother was pissed at him for scaring her like that, he just laughed and laughed. I was probably about three years old when that happened, but sometimes it feels like yesterday.

My father was only fourteen when his first child was born, and by sixteen, he had two sons. He and my mother were both in their late teens when they met and got married, then I came along. They were together until I was five but never got a divorce, and after she and I moved in with Papa and Oma, my father went his own way. For the first few years after they broke up, I would hear that song, "I Saw Mommy Kissing Santa Claus," during Christmas and pray for my parents to get back together. I'd be on my knees, just praying and praying—*God . . . Jesus, please bring my daddy back and let me find him kissing Mommy.* It's not like we ever had mistletoe hanging up in the house or anything, but I guess I just felt that she was my mother, he was my father, and we should all be together. That wasn't meant to be.

My father didn't live too far from us, and when I was eight years old, he and his new girlfriend had a son. We talked on the phone, and I'd also go see him at his place and spend time with my little brother. I loved all of my brothers, and when we were younger, my mother made sure we stayed connected. She would take me to see my older brother, who lived with his mother in the Bronx, and during the summer, she'd drive me upstate, where my oldest brother, my father's namesake, lived with his girlfriend and baby daughter. But as much as I was in touch with my siblings, the contact I had with my father gradually started to change. The phone calls seemed to be less frequent and his broken promises just kept coming. It was obvious that my mother had no tolerance for him, so Papa often stepped in to protect me from getting caught in the middle of their mess. If he noticed that I'd been outside waiting for my father a little bit too long, he would call me in, gently.

"Maybe he'll stop by while you're eating dinner," Papa would say. "Come on inside now, okay?"

If my father *did* show up, Papa was never disrespectful to him, nor did he ever call him names and whatnot. I'm sure he could sense that something was off, though. The fact was that my father was out in the streets, doing his thing and getting high. Eventually, my mother wound up doing the same thing.

By the time I was nine, my mother was an intravenous drug

user. She used to smoke marijuana and have a drink every now and again, but when she started dating a new man, who was Italian like my father, she really started partying. After about two years, she tried heroin for the first time. That's the story my aunt once told me. My grandparents were church-going folks, so I really don't think they knew what was going on with my mother, but I stumbled on the truth one day while I was watching the news. Heroin was really killing the streets at that time, and I remember seeing a report about a group of addicts up in Harlem. When they showed a close-up of one man's swollen hands, I recognized my *mother's* hands, right away. I think I was about twelve years old then, and I ran to tell my grandmother what I'd seen.

"Oma, Oma, I know why mommy's hands are that way," I said. "She takes some type of drug and sticks the needle in her hand."

She didn't seem to understand what I was talking about, but it was all beginning to add up for me. Even though I was still a kid, I could see what was going on, and it made me wise up. My father was still not around much, but I hadn't lost any love for him. I just stopped believing his promises. My normal became, *If he comes, it would be great to see him. If not, that's okay, too.* I accepted that he wasn't there, so I didn't get upset or feel the need to explain anything to anybody. That came later.

Dealing with my mother was a different story. Because she lived in the house with us, there was no hiding from the obvious. My friends used to ask me what was wrong with her hands, and I made up a story about her being in the Army Reserve and accidentally spilling acid on her hands, or something like that. I never knew what to say, so I lied because I didn't think people would understand.

The fact that both of my parents were on drugs could have been devastating, but it didn't affect me that way. I'd like to think that I came into the world with a strong constitution, but I also had a good upbringing. I grew up in a house filled with lots of love and constant words of encouragement. My grandparents made sure I stayed busy, so if I wasn't singing in the children's choir or playing with the bowling league, I was off doing activities with my Brownie and Girl Scout troops. There was a lot of church, too, and food and festivities. Oma cooked a big dinner *every* Sunday, and Papa, who drove elder church members back and forth to service, used to bake hams for funeral repasts. The foundation they created kept me grounded, and seeing how much they loved and supported each other really left an impression. Aside from providing a loving home, the greatest gift my grandparents gave me was making sure I had a relationship with God. They also taught me how to pray— and I *did*.

When I was a teenager, my father completely turned his life around. After many failed attempts, he'd admitted himself into a local treatment center and finally got clean. I'd visit him there and I remember how proud he was to introduce me to everybody.

"Come meet my daughter," he'd say. "This is *Simone*."

He used to love hearing people comment on how much we looked alike. I could see that he was as happy to see me as I was to see him, and he was also really optimistic about the future. Then he made me another promise.

"Daddy's getting his life together," he said. "When I get out of here, I'm going to be a father to you and your brothers."

I so wanted to believe him, and I *did* believe him. And for a long while, he did have it together. For the first time in years, he was present and dependable. He was working as a drug counselor, getting back on his feet, and sticking to his plan. It felt so good to be able to call him whenever I wanted, whether to ask for a few dollars to buy the latest sneakers or if I just wanted to hear his voice. He became my father, a provider, and a friend. And I really loved having him back.

We talked about everything. He told me about the abuse he endured as a child, which was at the core of the issues he was dealing with as a man. We talked about drugs and addiction and the fact that once you're an addict, you're always an addict. That's when I really began to understand that addiction is a disease. He also apologized for not being there for me when I was younger, and I forgave him. Deep down, I knew he was a good guy, with a kind heart, and because of that, I always had a great deal of compassion for him. I felt the same way about my mother, whom he loved very much and talked about all the time. Because they were still legally married, he wanted to help her get clean, too, so they could be together again and healthy. He really seemed to want to make things right.

My father was by my side when I gave birth to my first child. I was a scared, skinny nineteen-year-old, and he was right there with me. He was cracking jokes with my then-boyfriend and now-husband while I was going through labor. At one point, I looked over at him and thought, *Oh man, this is cool. My dad is here.* After all the time he'd missed, I was really happy to have him in my life for the important moments. That lasted for a while, but not long enough.

A year and a half after my son was born, and two weeks before I gave birth to my oldest daughter, my mother passed away. I was twenty-one. Whereas my father had gotten clean, my mother had continued to spiral downward into drugs and never made it out. Shortly after praying with Papa and asking for forgiveness, she slipped into a coma. It was a sad time for my family, but I felt a sense of relief just knowing that she was at peace. My father didn't handle it so well. Her death was really hard for him because it also meant the death of his dream for them to start over. But what really took him out was when his mother got seriously ill two years later. When Nana died, he completely fell apart and slowly began to slip back into his old habits. He was never the same after that.

He was living in the Bronx with his girlfriend when I noticed he was drinking. I'd taken the kids to spend the weekend with him, and as I was leaving, I saw him holding a beer. I was immediately concerned.

"Oh, don't worry, it's just a beer," he started to explain. "I'm good because . . ."

I can't remember what he said to try to convince me that everything was fine. I really wanted to believe him, even as I watched him sip on "just a beer" for almost a year. Then it all started again. There were days when I couldn't find him or wasn't able to reach him. That was my first indication that something might be wrong. My suspicions were confirmed soon after, when I asked him to drop the kids off at their grandmother's house. I made sure to pack everything they needed to spend the night, including clothes for the next day. I'd even bought them new coats as it was starting to get cold outside. Everything was fine, I thought. Then the phone rang.

"Simone, what are the kids going to wear tomorrow?" my soon-to-be mother-in-law asked. "Your father didn't drop off any clothes for them."

As I was in the middle of trying to explain that everything was inside of the bag I'd packed, I realized in an instant that he must have sold the kids' clothes. I was so embarrassed that I couldn't even think of what else to say. Like many people, she was aware of the history of my parents' drug abuse, so she was understanding and not judgmental. I was completely disgusted with my father, though, and when I finally got him on the phone, I cussed him out like never before. That's when I knew I needed to take a break from him.

When I got married, it was my grandfathers who walked me down the aisle. I was pregnant with my third child then and the one person missing that day was my father. He was just . . . out there, doing his thing, *again*. As much as I'd loved having him around, my life was moving on. I was a wife and the mother of two, then three, and ultimately four, and I had to consider the needs of my husband and children. Sadly, my older brother died of a rare blood disease a few days after my youngest was born, which had to have been really hard for my father, too. I wish I could have offered him some support, but I just didn't have the time or energy to keep up with whatever he was doing at the time. I continued to pray for him, though. I prayed for him all the time. Then I had another awakening.

When my son was ten years old, my father hurt his feelings so badly that it took me right back to the days when I used to wait and wait for him to walk down my block. He'd promised to come by and teach his grandson how to play the congas. Instead of following through, the phone calls and excuses started. I wasn't going to deal with that. Not anymore. And when he called to make just one more excuse, I let him have it as soon as I picked up the phone.

"Let me tell you something, motherfucker!" I screamed. "Remember all those days you had me waiting on the stoop and you never came? Well, you will *not* do that to my son because he *has* a father and a *great* grandfather. If you want to be in my kids' lives, you will be consistent. If you can't do that, then don't come around."

And I hung up.

My oldest daughter recently told me that she never understood why I seemed so angry when my father died in 2007. I had my reasons. I tried to be strong while making his funeral arrangements, but what nobody really knew was that when I was alone, I cried about him and what could have been. I cried a lot. When I think back to that afternoon when my cousin called to break the news to me, I remember having so many emotions. I was heartbroken. I was shocked and sad, too. And I was definitely angry, because my father didn't have to die.

After decades of drug addiction, he started to develop poor circulation in his legs. He'd been staying with his father in Brooklyn for a while and I'd take the kids to visit him a couple of times a year. One day my grandfather called to tell me that my father's legs had swollen up badly and were turning dark purple. He wasn't in good shape, nor was he doing anything about it, so I picked him up and took him to the doctor. That's when we found out that one of his legs was basically dead and needed to be amputated.

He was against it from the start.

"I was born with these legs, I'm going to die with these legs," he'd say whenever the subject came up.

"Daddy, you've got grandkids!" I told him. "Don't you want to be around for them? You can get a prosthetic leg and learn how to walk again. You could live to be eighty years old."

As much as I hoped he could be okay in the long run, he wasn't hearing me, or my oldest brother, or my uncles, when we pleaded with him to have the surgery. My husband and I even offered him help with his medical expenses. We all wanted him to live and be healthy again, but he wouldn't budge—not even when the doctor said that *not* having the surgery would make him susceptible to life-threatening complications, including blood clots. All I could think was, *After all those years of not being there for his kids, why would he want to miss out on having time with his grandchildren? Could he really be that vain . . . and selfish?*

My father and I spoke two weeks before he died. I was so mad at him. After I pleaded with him again, I stared yelling and scream- ing. I just couldn't believe that he would risk his life when he had a fighting chance to save himself and be around for his family. But he'd made his decision, and he paid for it with his life. That's why I was angry. He could still be here, he *should* still be here, but he chose not to be.

I have made peace with the fact that I can't change the past, but sometimes I look at my son and three daughters and realize just how different their lives have been. I wish I could have had what they have—a loving father who provides for his family, spends good-quality time with them, and most important, is present and consistent. I am forever grateful to Papa for stepping in and raising me into the woman I am today, but I really wish I'd had my father there, too.

My parents and grandparents are all in heaven now, but I feel their presence every day. I see them in the mirror, too, and in the faces of my children. And like those who knew and loved my father often tell me, there's so much of him in me—from my quick wit to my smile. People always comment on my smile.

"She sure does look like Renato," they say.

When I think about how far I've traveled since my days on 198th Street, I understand that while my father was flawed, the best parts of him, and of my mother, are what make me who I am. For that, I feel so, so blessed. And I am *here*. ■

The Girl at the Window

SARAH TOMLINSON

THE FIRST TIME I SAID NO TO MY DAD, I was sitting in his basement studio apartment near Boston. He was on his twin bed, his socks drying on the headboard behind him, talking eagerly as a way to delay the answer he feared was coming. He'd been diagnosed with prostate cancer two years earlier, and having opted to forgo the traditional treatments he'd been offered, he wanted me to loan him $1,000 to buy a three-month supply of healing herbs he'd found on the internet.

I nervously shifted in my chair, reminding myself why I had to say no. Never mind that he was a self-confessed gambling addict whose compulsion had ruined his life and planted landmines in mine. At thirty-seven, I was an up-and-coming author and ghostwriter whose own finances yo-yoed considerably. I only had the money he needed because I'd recently sold a memoir, *Good Girl*, that was about being abandoned by him. But always more mindful of my father's feelings than my own, I wasn't about to say anything that might hurt him. Instead, I opted for the gentle letdown.

"I'm sorry, Dad, but I can't give you the money," I said. "I don't want to jeopardize a relationship we've worked very hard to repair, when you're sick, by taking on too much responsibility for your treatment."

He was clearly disappointed, but he rebounded quickly. I followed his lead, allowing him to steer the conversation, as always.

When I drove away that evening, I was euphoric. I had stood up to the man who'd scarred my childhood with his absence and broken promises. That meant he couldn't hurt me anymore. And if *he* couldn't hurt me, then no one else could.

If only it were that simple.

In the months that followed, although his cancer did not seem to be progressing, it didn't go away, either. I saw an eventual end to our enmeshed relationship, whether we orchestrated it or the universe did.

Now, truly, was the time to face the legacy of our painful past, before it was too late. I had moments of success: I detached from any judgment of his treatment plan. I had moments when I relapsed, just like he did with the track. As when he told me that, *now*, he'd really quit gambling, when he'd only lied about it before, as a way to enlist my belief in—if not my financial support of—his alternative cancer approach. With practice, I got better at detaching from any expectations of *anything* from him. Still, I worried about him as if he was the child and I was the adult, while unable to stop craving his parental support, because that's what I'd always done.

I published *Good Girl*, a raw account of my lifelong quest for a relationship with my father and the self-destructive behavior I'd long engaged in to salve the lack his absence had created inside of me. He read every word, giving me the ultimate compliment when he compared my writing to his favorite writer: Jack Kerouac. He even apologized. And he even seemed to mean it.

With each new chapter in our story, I was sure I'd found the moment that would not only heal us, but finally heal me, fill in my lack, make me impenetrable to my father, my poor romantic choices, and all of the self-doubt that still plagued me.

And yet, even as I progressed, I continued to wobble. I continued to be the girl at the window I'd always been. That's where I'd waited for my dad as a kid, on the days he'd promised to visit me from Boston. Straining to see through the dense stands of trees that surrounded me, I sought a flash of bright yellow, the signal that his taxicab was heading up the driveway toward the house, toward me.

Fluttery with excitement and nerves, I calmed myself by doing math in my mind. It took three-and-a-half hours to drive from Boston to my mom's house in Midcoast Maine. If my dad had left at nine, he would be here at twelve thirty, one o'clock if he'd stopped for gas. I hadn't seen my dad in more than a year, and in that time, he'd made plans to visit me several times. And he'd always canceled at the last minute.

Still, I continued to believe, as I'd always believed, and as I would continue to believe for many years to come. If he was not here yet, the problem must be with my math, so I redid the numbers in my mind.

My mom passed in and out of the house, emptying the compost bucket, returning with fresh picked green beans for dinner. She smiled when I turned to watch her pour a glass of iced tea in the kitchen, but she didn't say anything to me about my dad. She let it be between him and me. Without an adult to warn me about the obstacles keeping my dad from me, I could only rely on what he told me. And so, on this day, he was coming to see me.

Finally, hours later, the phone rang. I did not give up my loyal post at the window, even as I struggled to hear what my mom was saying.

"Sarah, it's for you," she said, her voice tight in a way that would have upset me if she was angry at something I'd done. But I knew it wasn't me she was mad at.

I walked slowly to the phone, holding my body with careful precision, as if being perfect would somehow unlock my power, although everything about this day had made me feel anything but powerful. I clutched the plastic receiver tightly.

"Hi, Sarah," my dad said.

No one else said my name quite like him, with his particular lazy urban drawl, the legacy of his teenage years in the Trenton projects.

"Hi, Dad," I said, my tone as studied as my motions. Fearing I might scare him away, I carefully masked any sadness or anger.

"Bernie couldn't lend me a cab for the weekend," he said.

"Okay," I said.

"Okay" was my response to whatever my dad said. It seemed the safest.

I did not hang up on him or lie down on the floor and kick my feet or make even a single sound. My dad spun his excuses, never explaining why he'd let me burn with anticipation all day, instead of calling me earlier.

"I'll figure out when I can get up there again and I'll send a letter with the dates," he said, his tone brightening when he finally got to the promises: long drives and fish sandwiches at the place he liked on Route 1.

I could feel myself on the vinyl car seat next to my dad, breathing in the musky sweetness of the incense he burned in the ashtray, enraptured by his latest master lecture on reincarnation or astral projection or the benefits of a macrobiotic diet. I could taste the salty tang of tartar sauce on the fried fish sandwich. But I was exhausted after my day at the window, the place I spent more time waiting for my dad as a child than I ever actually spent with him. The tiniest doubt wriggled up.

"When?" I asked.

"I don't know, Sarah . . . as soon as I can," he said, his voice instantly stripped of lightness. "I have to go."

Worried my question was enough to frighten him, I repented and resumed my role as his biggest believer, best listener, and most loyal devotee.

"Okay," I said.

Between my mom leaving my dad when I was two and me leaving home early for college, my dad and I had dozens of telephone conversations like this. Meanwhile, my vigil at the window was rewarded with the appearance of his bright yellow taxicab in our driveway less than a dozen times.

And yet, I never stopped believing: in him or in the certain bliss of our eventual reunion. I elevated my dad above all others, viewing him like a touring rock star, and assumed that if he couldn't be with me, he must be busy with incredibly exciting matters elsewhere, despite all the evidence he gave me to the contrary: letting me sit in the backseat of the taxi he occasionally drove up to see me; taking me to the Boston race track he frequented enough to know all the regulars; describing at great length the latest affirmation, seminar, or book that was going to free him of his past limitations and allow him to achieve nothing short of complete enlightenment. I was too young to know that this triptych of taxi, track, and fruitless self-help was what had finally driven my mom to leave him in the first place.

They'd met at the Trenton Public Library, where my mom worked after college. My dad, who'd been expelled for truancy in ninth grade, was living with his mother following several years of hitchhiking the country like the Beat Generation writers he loved. They embarked on a passionate relationship and traveled up the coast, settling in Maine. The passion, as happens, wasn't always happy. They were on the verge of breaking up when my mom got pregnant with me. My dad asked her to marry him, but she said no, because, she later told me, she believed in marriage.

That summer, my dad left us at the remote farmhouse where

I'd been born, without a car, and hitchhiked down to Boston for a refresher course in est, a self-improvement seminar. He hoped it would make him the father he feared he couldn't be. Instead, he felt empowered to go to the track, where he won $100, and then lost it. For the next forty years, his gambling was the black hole that swallowed up everything around it.

During the years when I didn't see my dad, I grew up in what I can now see was an idyllic outpost in the woods of Maine. My mom and some friends had bought a hundred acres of land around the time my mom left my dad. She set off on this new life by herself, soon enlisting my stepfather to build a 740-square-foot, passive-solar, wood-heated house on their ten-acre plot, and create an existence based on the ideals of the back-to-the-land movement (sort of like a 1970s version of *Little House on the Prairie*, but with tofu and carob). My stepfather could not have been a better provider, literally building our house around us, and buying me a Cabbage Patch doll and my first Walkman. But he did not charm me like my father did during the rare interludes when Dad rolled onto the land with a waft of essential oils and a barrage of questions about my life and interests.

My dad seemed to want to know everything about me—to want to know the real me—and I couldn't resist the siren call of his attention. Sadly, I didn't have the critical faculties at age five or eight or thirteen (or thirty, honestly) to understand that the brief, sparkly promise of these visits would never be enough to compensate for the hours I'd lost waiting for him at the window, and the even greater number of hours I'd spent, post-puberty, pining after men I idealized and longed for, even though most of them were essentially strangers to me, because longing was how I showed love.

As a child, I came to equate my longing for my dad with a longing for his life in Boston, which I saw as much bigger and splashier than my own. By age eleven, I'd been alienated from my mother and stepfather by the birth of my half brother, and even from my beloved father by the birth of my half sister. Both siblings seemed to belong to complete families that did not include me. I now longed not only for my dad but also for independence. My dream was to live on my own, create my own equivalent of the glamorous life I imagined, and then befriend my dad.

Thanks to my mother's steadfast support (she had quietly been seeing the real me when I'd assumed my father was the only one with such superpowers), I was able to pursue my dreams of a big life by dropping out of high school and starting college at fifteen. During my first month of school, which was in Western Massachusetts, I did, in fact, go to Boston and see my dad while I was there. This time, though, we had a small disagreement about the type of kids I was hanging out with, and when my dad walked away from me, he would not see me for the next ten years.

During this time, my father sent me occasional letters and holiday cards, often with very specific, detailed plans for visits that he never actually made.

Some things hadn't changed.

Some things, however, had.

After our fight, my dad sent me a letter of apology in which he finally admitted his longtime struggle with gambling. From then on, when he made excuses for not visiting me, they contained elements of the truth—until he got his gambling in check, healed his bad back, and settled an ongoing lawsuit related to an automobile accident that had worsened his back, he didn't feel able to see me.

At first, I was thrilled about being invited into the adult world of my dad's real problems, which I'd been shielded from as a child. And then, I got frustrated. I wasn't the little girl at the window anymore. I had gone out to meet the world and decided I was a writer, an elusive passion that required a daily battle against procrastination and fear in order to face the page. I wanted desperately to succeed, to write something that mattered. And so I applied myself to my writing. But I also drank. A lot. And chased men who didn't return my feelings or, sometimes, even have a clear idea of who I was (ardent crushes from a distance being my particular specialty). I drank some more. And I doubted myself, no matter what success I began to achieve.

Always, I saw a gaping distance between who I was and who I wanted to be, and in that chasm, I saw my dad and all of the big wins that had never happened, the self-improvements that had never stuck. But after decades of total belief in his infallibility, I was equally terrified of really looking at him or taking him down from his pedestal and realizing I'd been worshipping the wrong man. Even though I'd literally left the window, a significant part of me was still there, waiting for him.

After I'd lived in Boston for a full year without once seeing my dad, I wrote him a letter telling him, "Don't wait until you're perfect, or it will be too late." I invited him back into my life, just as we were, at that exact moment in time. And remarkably, he heard me. He had lunch with me on his fifty-fifth birthday.

We began having regular dad-daughter dates, getting to know each other and, eventually, healing old wounds. During this time, my sister, now a teenager, also sent my father a letter. Having been raised in Bavaria after her German mother left our dad, she was curious about him and visited Boston. I was wary of her, jealous of the deep love Dad clearly felt for her. But I was also impressed by how clearly she saw him, saying during a brief moment we had alone: "He can be so much the child."

I had breakthroughs when I achieved insights into my dad's character and our relationship. And then, as always, I resumed my old, familiar role: the loyal daughter at the window, longing for more than he could give. Still, our relationship grew.

I moved to Los Angeles, pursuing my big life, striving to make it as a writer, finding some success. And yet, when it came to my dad, I continued to remain the little girl I'd always been. We hatched a plan whereby he was going to win $100,000 at the track, give me the down payment to buy a house, and then move into the guest-house. I read the books he recommended, watched the films he sent. I made stabs at independence and saw a therapist, who all but diagnosed my dad as a textbook narcissist and encouraged me, finally, to set boundaries. I did, and I didn't.

All of this continued through my dad's cancer and the release of my memoir, and through the first adult romantic relationship I'd managed to sustain in thirteen years.

And then, my sister, who I'd begun to build a relationship with, had a baby. My boyfriend and I traveled to Germany to see her and meet her boyfriend and son. I didn't have an agenda. I wasn't even sure we'd talk about our father, as the focus of the trip was on her new family.

Halfway through our visit, she and I sat by a magical Bavarian lake, sunlight and shadows dappling the pudgy thighs of her baby son. And we talked about where we had come from. Through her words, I saw that there could have been another way. There had been another way. Because our father had only visited her once during her childhood, she had never internalized his gambling or the codependent urges of the abandoned child. She had sometimes missed him, yes, and wondered where he was. But she had never waited at any window for him, literally or metaphorically. She had accepted that he was not there and was not coming. And although she had followed much the same path back to him, writing a letter to invite him back into her life, she had never believed that his absence had been because of any lack in her. She had never put his happiness above her own.

Gently, she coaxed me to love him, yes, to care about his well-being as he aged, but to truly detach from my impossible sense of responsibility for him. As I felt myself turn away from the window, the weight of all that longing rose up from me and floated off above the mountains, dispersing among the wisps of gentle cloud. ∎

I Was the Different One

NISA RASHID, AS TOLD TO THE EDITOR

MY BIRTHDAY IS IN APRIL, which is also National Poetry Month. In 2011, when I turned eleven, I decided to write eleven poems to celebrate both occasions. One of my poems, which I entitled, "While I'm Alive, I Will," read more like a bucket list. It included eight things that I hoped to do before I die, like ride a unicorn to Alaska, marry my love on a Mediterranean wave, and even dye my hair neon green. I also wrote that I wanted to walk a Brooklyn street with my father.

I was so young when I wrote that poem. I was optimistic and tended to fantasize about what might be possible, especially when it came to my father. Back then, I didn't really understand what deportation meant. I didn't realize that when he was sent to Guyana in 2009, when I was nine, it meant that he would not be allowed to come back to the United States. If he wasn't allowed to come back to the States, then he wouldn't be able to stop by his old block in the Bronx, and he definitely couldn't come see me in Brooklyn. I also didn't know that there was another option—that I could visit him in his homeland and walk down a street with him there.

I always knew that he had been in prison, but I was never embarrassed about him being my father. What was embarrassing for me was knowing that my friends and I didn't have the same type of home lives. A lot of them lived with their dads, and because I sometimes talked about mine, they'd ask me why he was never around when they came over. I didn't know how to answer their questions, so I'd always find a way to make light of the fact that he wasn't there at *that* moment. I knew I was the different one, which was hard for me to admit and accept when I was a little girl.

When I was seven, my mother and I went out with a friend of mine, along with his mother. While we were eating, our mothers shared that both of our fathers were serving time in prison. I immediately felt a sense of relief. Before that day, I had no idea that there were other people, and definitely not somebody I knew, in the same situation. Knowing that I wasn't alone helped me feel much more comfortable talking about my father.

As much as I used to avoid going into detail about his whereabouts, my father being in prison was never really a secret. My mother had written books and articles about their relationship, about our life, so many people knew the story. When I was growing up, I don't remember anybody talking about him or the situation too much, though. My mom's friends might ask, "Oh, how's your dad doing?" or something like that, but nobody ever asked me questions like, "Oh my God, how does it feel to not have a father?" Sometimes I would feel bad that he wasn't with me, physically, but I never felt like I didn't have a father. We have a great relationship and he's always had a very strong presence in my life. I've always had my father.

I haven't seen him, in person, for a while, not since before he was deported, but we are still very close. We talk twice a week, and also stay in touch through social media. We Skype sometimes, too. I still remember when my mother and I would wake up early to drive or take the bus to go visit him. For me, those were always such happy times because I got to see him and spend time with him, but my mother used to tell me how mean the officers were to her, especially when I was a baby. She'd tell me that they were really horrible to her and made her feel uncomfortable during those visits, but I don't remember any of that.

My mother didn't tell me everything about his incarceration when I was growing up, but I think she was as honest as she could be. Even though she didn't outright say why he was serving a twenty-year sentence, she never painted him as a criminal either. Instead, she'd talk about the type of man he was. She always told me that he was a good person and that he didn't have the proper support or guidance around him when he was younger. That, along with his surroundings, was a big part of the reason why he was sent to prison as a teenager. He's made that clear to me, too.

If I had to describe my father in a few words, I would say that he is very protective and extremely caring. He always tells me how much he loves me, and as I'm maturing, he talks to me about boys—"Be careful!"—just as any father would with his daughter. He sees my grades and hears all about my accomplishments from my mom, but one of the hardest and most confusing things about not living under the same roof with him is that he hasn't been able to see me grow, firsthand. I can tell that he knows I'm doing well because he always reminds me that I'm a smart, beautiful young lady. He's very encouraging and always wants the best for me. I know that, too.

I should also mention that my father is really religious. He grew up Catholic, but converted to Islam when he went to prison, before he and my mother got married. When I was born, I was given two Arabic names—Nisa means "the woman" and Rashid means "the guide"—but I don't identify as Muslim, which is something I've expressed to him. He has tried to tell me that having one parent who is Muslim technically makes *me* Muslim, too, but I don't agree with him about that. As much as I respect his choice, I don't like some of the practices of his religion, especially as it relates to sexism. I know that Muslim women are supposed to cover their hair and things like that, but I don't support that. My mother is much more liberal and understanding.

We might not see eye-to-eye on religion, but my father and I are definitely connected by culture. His family is from Guyana, so like him, I strongly identify with Guyanese culture. Living in New York, where so many cultures are appreciated, I am surrounded by Caribbean people in my neighborhood, and I am also in touch with my roots through food and music. I've taken it upon myself to read about Guyana and study its history, and my mom says that when I'm sixteen, we can take a trip so that I can see the country for myself. I look forward to that, but most of all, I look forward to seeing my father and walking down the street with him, hand in hand. I think we'll both be happy on that day. Until then, I will try to stay open and optimistic.

Growing up with a parent in prison was not an ideal situation, but as I get older, I understand how important it is to work with what you have. As thankful as I am to have such a wonderful father, I also know that it wasn't easy for my mother to carry so much of the weight of taking care of me. I appreciate her for all she's done, and while we've had help from my grandparents and many friends, I think that running a household and raising a child is too much for one person to take on.

A lot of people ask me about my outlook on marriage and family, and I always say that I'd definitely like to have both. I see myself being married in the future and my husband will be at *home*. That last part is non-negotiable. Maybe I'll even marry my love on a Mediterranean wave, just as I'd envisioned when I eleven years old, when I wrote that poem. We shall see. ∎

II. Divorced

What's in a Name?

TAMALA MERRITT, AS TOLD TO THE EDITOR

I HAVE TO CREDIT MY HUSBAND for implementing the "no D-word" rule in our marriage. We're both products of divorce, and while my mother moved on and married my stepfather, whom I've called Dad since I was seven years old, my husband's father left his mother during his freshman year of college and married the neighbor with whom he'd been having a twenty-year affair. Because he felt that his parents' marriage was a lie, my husband refuses to leave that legacy for our daughter and two sons to carry. He's a big proponent of working things out—no matter the issue, every time—and I respect him for that. I really do.

When we got married nineteen years ago, I couldn't wait to go to the social security office to get my paperwork in order. Honestly, I have never understood the concept of hyphenating. To me, attaching your married name to your maiden name is like trying to hold on to a piece of the past, which is the opposite of what I wanted. I suppose there are some people who might have a strong connection to who they used to be, but my thought was, *I'm ready to be somebody different.* I couldn't wait to start life anew, with my new name. It's something I'd been waiting to do for a very long time.

The definition of family can be tricky. Experience has taught me that your family is the group of people with whom you build a life and create memories. They are the ones who really care about you. In my case, I've come to understand and accept that sharing genes with someone doesn't make them your family, especially if they're not present in your life. That's how I would classify my father.

My mother and father were once married, but other than the fact that their union didn't last very long, I don't know much about their relationship. By the time I was six months old, my mother had left him in Texas and returned to her hometown in Oklahoma, with me in tow. I have seen my father twice since then—the summer I was six and then four years after that. Both times, I naively believed that he'd sent for me, but when I arrived, I was surprised to discover that he had little interest in me. As a child, I sensed that I was just an afterthought to him, as if he could take me or leave me. While it was certainly obvious that my grandmother—his mother—wanted to see me, and was *happy* to see me, I remember feeling invisible in his presence.

Over the years, I've heard rumblings about how my father abused my mother and abused himself with alcohol and drugs. My mother always jokes, "He didn't give you much, but you got some of his good genes," when referring to the slender physique I inherited from my father. She never said much else, nor did she speak badly of him, but it didn't take very long for me to figure things out for myself.

I would learn much later that he never paid her a dime in child support, but he did attempt to save money to enter the fast food business. As the story goes, he remembered that I liked the roast beef sandwiches at Arby's, so he wanted to invest in a franchise, for me. As a kid, I remember thinking, *That's the dumbest shit in the world.* He was remarried by then, with another daughter, and his wife told me that I should try to be more supportive of his dreams. When I told my mother, she said, "Oh, I remember him always talking about his dreams." And that's all he would ever do—dream and talk. He never did the work. In my mind, he was a loser.

Back in Oklahoma, my mother met a wonderful man who would become my stepfather. I call him Dad because he *is* my dad. When they got married, my mother took his last name, but I kept my father's name. Looking back, I suppose that a trip down to the courthouse, coupled with the fees involved in filing the paperwork for a voluntary name change, for a minor, was not a top priority. On the flip side, one family with members having two last names, living under one roof, often required some explaining. There were a number of awkward situations at school when someone would mistakenly address my dad by my father's last name. He always handled it calmly, but I was embarrassed by it.

I didn't want to carry my father's name.

Because my home life was stable and happy, I didn't miss my father or feel sad that he wasn't around. I definitely didn't feel like I was lacking in any way, either. I blocked out the first seven years of my life and pretended that my two-parent family had always been as it was. Seeing my mom and dad together was important for me. They were my foundation. It's not that they were over-the-top affectionate, but I knew theirs was a relationship built on love and mutual respect. Also, my dad was a hardworking man who took care of his family, which, much later, would also include my sister, who came along when I was in college. Together, they showed me what being a family unit was all about and provided me with a great example of what was possible. It's when we ventured out of the house that things got more complicated.

Of the three families I was connected to—two by blood and another by marriage—I was only embraced by one. To this day, it's my mother's family that showers me with affection. With them, I always feel whole and welcome. With my father's family, I felt like a guest because, after all, I only visited them twice. It was within my dad's extended family, however, that I felt like a complete outsider. The adults didn't make it very easy for me—especially his mother. In her house, I was made to feel like a stepchild. She made sure of that.

My dad's family was huge, with lots of aunts, uncles, and cousins. There were eighteen grandchildren, if you count me, and I remember there were always big, elaborate Sunday dinners. But when the holidays came around, spending time with them was especially difficult. Every Christmas, my dad's mother gifted all of the kids with cash. That was her tradition. Every envelope would have a name written on the front and inside there would be a crisp $100 bill. Except for mine. Inside the envelope with my name on it was a $50 bill, always. That was her not-so-subtle way of reminding me that I was not her blood, and it hurt my feelings, every year, because I so badly wanted to belong. My mother was not happy about this and spoke up about it often, but I felt bad for my dad, because I knew he was caught in the middle. If I could go back to those times, I would remind myself that there were people who loved me and thought I was special. Those were the people I needed to concentrate on and invest my faith and trust in. They were the ones who deserved my energy. Connection is a two-way street.

Aside from those two trips I'd taken to Texas, I didn't have any contact with my father. There were no birthday cards or anything, but he did call to congratulate me when I earned my undergraduate degree. I didn't think much of the conversation, but when he referred to me as "doctor," I realized just how little he knew about me and what was going on in my life. I held my tongue, but I really wanted to ask, "How does having a bachelor's degree make me a *doctor*?" I went on to earn my master's degree and wasn't surprised when I didn't hear from him. Even though he had no understanding of my academic achievements or my life goals, I found it ironic that it would be *his* last name to appear on both of my degrees. While I was certainly proud of the work I'd put in, I didn't want any of what I did to be associated with him.

Aside from my overwhelming desire to change my last name, I always knew I wanted to be married and have children. My husband and I met in college, and although we knew each other through friends, we didn't get together until after we'd graduated. In him, I saw many of the qualities I admired in my dad. He was hardworking, thoughtful, loving, and most important, he was and wanted to be *present*. That was the example my dad had set for me. Also, we had similar goals, one of which was to leave the Midwest, where we'd graduated from college, as soon as we could. That last part didn't work out as planned. Instead, we've built a family in a city without our extended family, but with a network of friends who *feel* like family. We live in our own little cocoon, of sorts.

Our life is good, but I have not been totally truthful with my family. In short, my three children know nothing about my father. They believe that my dad is their biological grandfather. They would have no reason not to. He is their granddad, *period*. When my eldest son, who's now a teenager, was old enough to read and ask questions, I took the two frames holding my degrees off of the wall. I didn't want to explain why my maiden name didn't match that of my mom and dad. I'm not ashamed of the facts, but because I've been open and honest about everything else, I knew that I'd be honest with them if they asked why my name is different. At the time, I wasn't ready to have those conversations, so I put the frames away. I like the life I've created and I don't want to rock the boat, not just yet. One day, I will. They should know the truth, and I will tell them when the time is right, when I'm ready to tell the stories. That day is coming soon.

A few years ago, my half sister—my father's daughter—found me on Facebook, and we've been in touch sporadically, but nothing substantial has come of our exchanges. I was struck, though, when she admitted that she wished he had been more present in her life. That's when I realized that it wasn't just me. Now that I'm an adult and a parent, I understand that it is my responsibility to make sure my kids have what they need and feel loved and protected. My father did none of those things. I have accepted that and choose to leave it in the past.

I certainly wish my father the best, wherever he may be, but I am thankful and grateful to have learned the difference between a father and a dad. My father is a man that didn't step up to be present and care for his family. My dad is the man who raised me, provided for me, and loved me as his own. He's the one who was there.

I'm still in the midst of family life and some days, the future seems so far away. Right now, the days are long and it's not always easy to juggle marriage, career, and children, but we're here and we're making it work. Watching my husband with the kids reminds me of how happy I am that we chose to walk this path together. He's a great dad, a great provider, and I have to smile when I see how he interacts with them, especially our daughter, who has him wrapped around her fingers. That is beautiful to see.

Like most parents, my hope for my children is that they be happy and find their place in the world. I want them to be of service to others, too. When I think about how they'll change as they build their own lives and families, I hope that they use us as a blueprint. I'll be honored if they say, "Wow, I really want what Mom and Dad have." ∎

Redefining Family

REGINA KING, AS TOLD TO THE EDITOR

Not long after my divorce was finalized, I spotted my ex-husband at one of our son's basketball games. He'd always been a present father, so it wasn't unusual for him to come out and show his support. I can't say that I was happy about him being there, though. Actually, I was still pissed about some of the messiness that had gone down during our breakup, so I really wasn't in the mood to see him at all, anywhere. Then something clicked.

At one point, I looked up and across the stands and realized that I was sitting on one side and he was all the way on the other. *Damn.* On an occasion when we should have been united, we were miles apart, which was not cool. I caught myself repeating a familiar pattern, and I should have known better. Because of our issues, Ian was becoming the kid whose parents were so disconnected that they couldn't even sit next to each other, let alone have a civilized conversation. I had been that kid once and it wasn't fun.

As soon as the game was over, I found my ex in the crowd and asked if he had a few minutes to talk. I really wanted to tell him how I was feeling, right in the moment. I wanted us to at least *start* the conversation, face-to-face.

"You know what? This is not good for Ian," I said. "Let's put this shit behind us, because it has nothing to do with how much we both love him."

He heard me out and after taking a deep breath, he agreed. I think we were both relieved to be taking the first step toward releasing the heaviness we'd been carrying around. That was our turning point.

It wasn't easy, but we started putting in the work it took to find our way back to a friendship. But even if we hadn't come back together—as friends or as parents—I never had any doubt about his role as a father. As he'd demonstrated at that basketball game and in so many other ways, he was front and center for Ian, who was in seventh grade then. That's the kind of father he'd always been. Unfortunately, my father wasn't that way.

I was only eight when my parents got divorced, but I don't remember their split being such a surprise. I never knew what went wrong, but after seven years, their relationship had reached a level where they were constantly arguing. Like, *every* day. There was a lot of door-slamming going on, too, and it was hard not to notice my dad sleeping in the living room. I remember him lying on the floor every night, for months, because the couch was too soft for his back. The tension was thick, and I was so embarrassed by the thought of everybody in the neighborhood knowing, or at least *hearing*, what was going on in our house. Although I wanted things to be different, my dad leaving the house was not the change I was hoping for.

There are moments that play back in my mind like a scene from a movie, and the day he told me and my sister, Reina, about the divorce is one of them. I can still see him sitting on the couch, picking us up, one by one, and placing us on either side of his lap. She and I were facing each other, looking up at him, as he began to explain why he was moving out. Reina is four years younger than me, so I doubt that she understood what he was saying, but I did. Well, I thought I did. He assured us that it wasn't such a big deal, that everything was going to be okay. I was relieved when he said his presence in our lives wouldn't change and that he'd still be around for us. Because of what he said that day, I figured that whatever was happening was just between my parents.

The word "divorce" wasn't foreign to me. As a child of the 1970s, I grew up as part of a generation of kids whose parents got divorced, and it wasn't seen as this terrible thing. Maybe that's why I believed what my father told me and Reina that day, that everything would be okay. But it wasn't. My parents' conduct during and after their divorce—from the constant fighting to their eventual estrangement—was very disappointing and hurtful to me. I was more disappointed and even more hurt when my father seemed to just drift out of our lives. I only realized much later that the divorce really had little to do with that. It had more to do with who he was as a man.

I've held on to the good memories I have of my dad. He'd take me and Reina to the drive-in movie, which we loved, and I remember him being the "fun dad" on our street. He was strong and lean back then; all of the kids thought they could outrun Mr. King, but they never could. He got a kick out of that. My dad was a handsome man and I always thought he had the most beautiful hands. As a mechanical engineer, he used his hands for work, but because he had two older daughters from his first marriage, he really knew how to comb hair, too! Whenever he did my hair, I just thought it was the coolest thing. I also remember the cross he wore around his neck. He wore it so much that I can still see the emerald stone that was in the center of it. That all feels like a lifetime ago.

After my dad moved out, Reina and I saw him pretty regularly. He lived in an apartment not too far from our house and we'd stay with him every other weekend. I don't remember the specifics about those weekends, but there were times when I played with a couple of kids who lived in his building. Their father was kind of mean and nasty, and I used to think, *Oh man, I'm so glad I have an awesome dad.* I felt lucky.

He never said anything about my mom and she didn't speak badly about him. It was only once I got older that she told me about him being late with child support or not paying any at all. Back then, though, the only thing she said was how our clothes smelled like cigarettes when we came back from visiting him. She'd quit smoking, but he hadn't yet, so she'd make us hang our clothes outside to get rid of the smell. But really, neither of them said much about the other, and when I think about it now, I wonder if they ever really spoke to each other much after the divorce. I'm sure they must have talked about when to pick us up and drop us off on those weekends, but that was probably about it.

Then there was a shift. I can't pinpoint when or how it started, but somewhere along the way, my dad just drifted away. Those every-other-weekend visits slowed down, too, but I didn't notice it right away because life was getting really busy at our house. Reina and I had been taking acting classes for a few years and by the time I was thirteen, we were both working on television. It was an exciting time for us, but our dad wasn't around very much. I can count on one hand the number of times he came to any of our tapings. That was definitely upsetting, but I never spoke up about it. I guess I just hoped things would somehow get better.

I credit my former costar Hal Williams with being a wonderful influence. He played my father on *227*, which aired for five seasons, and also became a father figure for me when the cameras stopped rolling. He'd let me sit up under him and talk about teenage stuff and just *be*, which was something I no longer did with my dad. Hal is a warm, loving person and I always appreciated him for being there for me. Around that time, I also had to deal with the fact that my dad married a woman who was barely five years older than me. At seventeen, that was a lot for me to process because, more than anything, I just wanted to be closer to him.

A lot of people think that girls need their mothers and boys need their fathers, but kids need *both* of their parents. Girls need their dads in their lives for so many reasons. There are certain things about life and relationships that only a father can teach his daughter. When he's not available to her, she ends up learning by trial and error. Tradition suggests that men are the "chasers," but that's only half of the story. We, as women, are the "choosers." We are the ones who get to say "yay" or "nay" to our suitors, but if a father, or another male figure, is not there to be an example for a young girl, how does she learn and sharpen her choosing skills? Many of us learn the hard way. I know I did.

Sometimes it's just about knowing that your father has your back, even if he doesn't speak a word. I remember being so hurt and upset when I broke up with my first boyfriend. That first real heartbreak is always painful, and the fact that I questioned myself so much made it even worse. *Was it me? Would he have been more interested if I looked like this or that? Did I say or do something to make him turn away?* Thankfully, Hal was able to console me, so I wasn't really thinking about my dad too much during that emotional time. Although I was long past the point of voluntarily sharing something so personal with him, in hindsight, I wonder if that experience might have settled differently if he'd been there supporting me. I doubt if I would have been sitting on those negative feelings about myself if he'd been there to just hug me and tell me I was going to be okay. Maybe I would have made different choices later on, too, but I'll never know.

Just as the details of the day he told us about the divorce are etched in my mind, so is the day my dad told me, Reina, and our older sister Pat about his Parkinson's diagnosis. We went to his house, and once we all sat down, he started to explain some of the strange things that had been going on. He told us about the time he stepped off of a curb and the edge of the pavement looked like it was ten feet tall. Then he told us about trying to walk through doorways and how everything would get warped and distorted. At first, he'd tried to brush those things off as signs of aging, but his friends urged him to go to the doctor. My sisters and I sat there in shock, looking back and forth at him and each other. We didn't know what to think or what to say.

I was completely in the dark about Parkinson's disease. I didn't know what it was or how it would affect his life, but just the thought of him facing a serious health issue was heartbreaking to me. And things only got worse. He deteriorated more and more, year after year. By the time the disease really began to take over his mind and body, he was living in Panola County, Texas, with his fourth wife. I was pregnant when my husband and I went to visit him, and I was devastated by what I saw. The house was so unkempt and seeing my dad living in those conditions made me even more emotional than I already was. My husband didn't want me to be in that environment, nor did he like seeing me so upset, so he made up an excuse for us to cut the trip short. I couldn't get that whole scene out of my head, though, and once I learned that my dad's son-in-law had stolen a lot of his money, I knew something had to change. That's when Pat and I started planning to bring him back home to Los Angeles.

Pat did the physical part of taking care of him and I handled the financial end. It wasn't easy for any of us; again, my emotions were all over the place. I loved my dad and did all that I could to make sure he had the best care, but I also felt some resentment about the situation. There were times when I thought, *You weren't there for me for so long and now I've got to take care of you?* Then, on the flip side, I felt guilty about being resentful toward someone who was suffering so much.

While we were caring for him, Pat and I really had a chance to talk, and I was surprised to hear that my dad hadn't been there for her or our other sister, LaVelle, in the ways that I'd always imagined. Ironically, both of us had believed that the *other* sisters had it better, but that wasn't necessarily the case. It was during one of our talks that Pat offered her perspective on my dad. She wondered if he was just old-school in his thinking, like maybe he believed that once kids got to a certain age, they were on their own and did their own thing. Her explanation was interesting. It also made me think that my father sort of placed a tattoo over a tattoo and just moved on. Perhaps that's just how he lived and who he was—for better or worse.

Although by this point he was not able to speak well or express his feelings, I sensed that he felt guilty about how things had turned out. I'm sure he had regrets about the past. I could see it on his face. I had regrets, too. I regretted the number of years that had passed without us having a better relationship. I regretted that he wasn't able to share in the special moments like my wedding, where my grandfather walked me down the aisle, or the birth of my son or any of my professional achievements. I also wished Ian could have had the opportunity to really know him. Sometimes he'd come with me to visit my dad, and I could tell that he didn't really know what to say. My mom had since remarried and it would be my stepfather who assumed the role of Ian's grandfather. I never got over the pain of my dad's departure from my life, but once the disease took over, I had no choice but to accept that he just couldn't be there for me—or any of us.

I was married for nine years before my husband and I separated and eventually divorced. Just as I'd watched my parents arguing and fighting, my son watched *his* parents arguing and fighting. It was like history repeating itself, and I felt terrible about him having to witness that. It was such a stressful time in my life, and although I was thankful to have my mother by my side, I also wished that I could have been able to pick up the phone and talk to my dad. He was just too ill by then, though. When I needed an ear, I talked to my girlfriends, many of whom had gone through divorces, too. Some of them even told me about how their fathers had helped them through and I realized, again, just how much I'd missed out on. I was a grown woman, yet I was still wishing my dad could be there for me, just as I had when I was a teenager.

He was eighty years old when he lost his battle with Parkinson's and I think about him often, especially when I hear a Michael Jackson song. They died during the same summer, in 2009, just months apart. My father is still so much a part of me—from my physique and fast metabolism, which I'm *so* thankful for now, to my sense of connection to the universe. As an adult, I found out that he'd introduced my mom to Religious Science all those years ago. We'd always gone to church with her, so I had no idea that he was the one who'd lead us down that path. That was a good feeling. I'll never know what my life would have been like if he'd been more available when I was growing up, but I don't feel any bitterness. Instead, I find myself still thinking about the would-haves, could-haves, and what-ifs.

It's kind of crazy to think that I've now been divorced longer than I was married, but I appreciate the journey, because it brought my ex and I back to a friendship that helped us become great co-parents. Ian's in college now and I know how much he appreciates us for making the effort, because he remembers when things were not so good. I'm just glad that we all made it to the other side. We've redefined what it means to be a family, *our* family, and we're all better for it.

As much as I always wished my dad had stuck around, it's such a blessing to see that Ian has a father who is there for him, no matter what. Sometimes when I catch him doing or saying something that reminds me of his dad, my heart just smiles because I know that he'll never feel disconnected from his father as I did with mine. That makes it all worth it. ■

Love, Peace, and Happiness . . . Despite My Father

CINDY M. BIRCH

So shall my word be that goeth forth out of my mouth:
it shall not return unto me void,
but it shall accomplish that which I please and
it shall prosper in that thing whereto I sent it.
ISAIAH 55:11

I AM A MIRACLE.

Despite the ugliness I witnessed and endured as a girl, I have no doubt that God has always been with me. I know that He did more than just bring me through a troubled childhood, too. God protected my spirit and my heart from being hardened and destroyed by some of the experiences I shared with my father.

There was a time when my wounds were deep, but I do not wield the sharp-edged sword of bitterness or revenge. Though I once felt abandoned, I don't wear the protective armor of mistrust and aloofness, either. In fact, I still believe in love and marriage *and* good men. I know that I will love and be loved by a faithful and Godly man before my soul leaves this world.

Yes, I am a miracle.

When I was six years old, I had a strong desire to know God and Jesus, but I had to sneak to church—with my mother's permission, of course. At the time, my understanding was that my father didn't want me to attend a Baptist church. I assumed that he wanted me to be Catholic because his family had roots in that denomination, but I felt more comfortable and uplifted in a lively Baptist service. Now that I'm an adult, I recognize the parallels between my fight to develop my spiritual faith and to hold tight to my faith in love. My father was a hindrance in both struggles.

During my early childhood, he was my playmate, my teacher, my champion, and my hero. From the day I was born until I turned six, I was a consummate daddy's girl. My father was very loving and playful with me then. He always told me that I was beautiful and smart and often bragged about my accomplishments to his friends and associates. My father taught me how to play chess and Scrabble at the age of four. An intelligent man who loved to learn, he taught me some algebra at that young age, too. Between my father and mother's homeschooling efforts, I entered kindergarten knowing how to read, count, add, subtract, and multiply. I remember feeling very confident, in every way.

Along with everything he taught me, I always felt that I understood my father better than anyone else. That's probably because he communicated with me in a way that he didn't, or couldn't, with adults. I was like a sounding board. He likely felt free to express some of the difficult things that happened during his life because he knew I couldn't really understand anyway. Through my little-girl comprehension, what I was able to grasp from our talks was that he was a hurting soul. Among his recollections were stories of abuse and tough times when he was growing up in the South Bronx. It all made me feel like he needed me in ways that my mother didn't.

"I know Cindy will take care of me," my mother said one day, rather matter-of-factly, about how she envisioned her golden years. She was talking to one of her friends, in front of me.

"I have to take care of my daddy," I declared, without a second thought. "He's gonna need me more than you."

In an instant, I sensed how those words hurt her feelings, but that wasn't my intention. Even as a kid, I recognized my mother's strength and stability. I always knew she would be fine, but I could see a not-so-easy future for my father. In him, I saw frailty and a lack of judgment.

I was almost seven when he ceased being my hero. I don't remember how the situation was ignited, but I do remember that there was yelling, manhandling, and a swinging pot in the air. Then I watched as my father literally dragged my mother down the hallway and into the master bedroom. I followed them, only to have the door slammed and locked in my face. I'll never forget the horror of hearing my mother screaming in pain, nor will I forget the sound of her body being flung against the walls and furniture. As much as I wanted to get to her, to protect her, all I could do was wait outside the door, silently screaming and jumping up and down. I was terrified.

Although I don't recall any earlier incidents of violence in our home, I must have witnessed *something*, because I knew right then that I was supposed to stay out of it. That knowing was confirmed when my father suddenly stopped brutalizing her and swung open the bedroom door. He immediately snatched me up.

"*Didn't* I tell you to mind your business?" he yelled in my face, before walking me to the front door and locking me outside on the porch.

On that day, we became enemies, my father and me. No longer could I be his ally. I was afraid of him, afraid that he might one day kill my mother. I was also afraid that he might brutalize me, too.

I don't know if it was as a result of that incident or the fact that I'd reached an age of understanding, but I began to see my father in whole. He was the loving, playful, encouraging, intelligent, talented man, yes, but he was also the adulterer, the liar, the selfish person, the brutalizer, the terrorist. Perhaps he was unaware, or simply chose to ignore it, but a rift began to spread wide between us. It was a divide that I would never be able to cross again, not completely.

When I was ten, my mom left him for good. I had encouraged her to leave and was thrilled when she finally did. We moved in with one of her sisters in the next town over. To keep from disrupting my fifth-grade year, my mother drove me to school in our old neighborhood and picked me up from a babysitter's house in the evening. I was usually careful not to walk near our old house, where my father still lived, but then came the day when I ran into him while I was with my friends. I guess I was closer to the house than I thought.

He was riding in the passenger seat of his friend's car when he spotted me. As soon as he caught my eye, I saw him tell his friend to pull over. Then he got out and walked over to me.

"Come on and go with me, Cindy," he said.

"No. Mommy told me not to go with you," I said, scared.

My father repeated himself and I refused, more adamantly. He looked hurt and embarrassed as his friend and my friends looked on in disbelief. He reached for my arm and I ran, screaming.

"Noooo! Mommy told me not to," I screamed. "Noooo!"

He chased me down the street, back up the street, and in circles as my friends chanted, "Go, Cindy! Go!"

When my father finally caught me, he smacked me hard on the butt, then took me inside the house and made me go to my old room. After he demanded that my uncle, who was living with him at the time, not allow me to leave, he left the house and just continued on with his day. Later, my friends came back and stood under my bedroom window, promising to bust me out of there, but because I was raised to be obedient to my parents, I was too afraid to try to escape. One of my regrets from back then is that I didn't know how to fight harder.

The same house that had once been my safe and happy home became a dark, dreary dungeon. For the next month, it's also where my father held me hostage. That's how I saw it, anyway. That's how it felt. As time marched on, my fears about him causing me physical harm began to subside a bit. He cried after the one spanking he gave me, saying that it hurt him more than it hurt me. So, I processed the fact that since he could brutalize my mother without remorse, his problem was with *grown* women. What worried me, though, was overhearing a conversation he had with a friend during which he threatened to take me out of the country so my mother would never see me again. That's when things became very icy between us.

He would only allow me to see my mother when she brought me clothes for school. Each time I went to meet her in the driveway, I asked why I couldn't just hop in the car and go with her. She told me that I had to wait, that she would work it all out with her lawyer and we'd be together again soon. Sure enough, I was called to the principal's office one day, and when I walked in, there was my mother! I was ecstatic when she said I'd be leaving with her immediately and would never have to go back to the house with my father.

After that day in the principal's office, I never returned to that school, and I didn't see my father again for thirteen years. I spoke to him on the phone a few times, but when I realized that he would continue to cause hardship to my mother, I told him he had to stop or he couldn't be in my life. He didn't call or try to contact me again until much, much later.

In the beginning, I wasn't too upset about not being in contact with him. Instead, I was just so grateful to feel safe and have peace at home. I also thrived at my new school and worked hard at all of my endeavors because I wanted to succeed. Although I didn't think I had anything to prove to my father, I started to feel bad about all of the things he was missing out on—from my Honor Society induction and student council presidential win to my recitals and my crowning as Miss Teen Model of New Jersey. Those were such special moments, but he wasn't there to share in any of them.

There were plenty of times when I was upset about the way he'd broken up our family. But as much as I wanted to hate him for abusing my mother and manipulating me, I just couldn't do it. I didn't choose him, but he was still my father, and very much a part of me. I felt connected to him because he'd instilled such a strong sense of family in me. Plus, everyone said I looked so much like him. When I looked in the mirror, I saw him, too, which made me feel for my mother. She was reminded of him whenever she saw me.

During the years I didn't see or hear from him, I often wondered if he was still alive. I had imaginary conversations with him and wrote poems about him to express my disappointment, anger, and resentment. He'd been an inspiration for my earliest poetry style, as I had memories of reading *his* prose. I always remembered his birthday, too, even when I tried to forget. He had done some good in my life, and although I didn't excuse the pain he'd inflicted on us, I still empathized with him, because someone or something from his past had twisted him to such a point. As his fourth oldest, I hoped that he was at least being a better father to his other children, which today total thirteen. I also forgave him for not being a father to me.

I had just turned twenty-four when my father contacted me again. Following a recent move and while sifting through old papers and photos, I found a slip of paper with his godmother's phone number written on it. Immediately, I felt compelled to call. I suppose I wanted to satisfy my curiosity. I wanted to know that my father was alive and well. I didn't want the next time I saw him to be in a casket.

A man I didn't know answered the phone. He said he hadn't seen my father in a while, but he took down my number, just in case. A month later, I answered my phone and heard a familiar voice.

"Hello, baby. How have you been?"

Any joy I might have felt from hearing my father's voice after so long soon melted into sadness and concern. He told me that I had a baby sister and brother in foster care and asked me to accompany him for weekly visits. He also asked if I would consider filing for custody of them, and within seconds, that strong sense of family took over. I barely heard what he said next because I was already making plans in my head. I was also thinking about *our* relationship and wondering where he'd been for so long, but I didn't question him about that in the moment. Soon after we talked that day, I met him at his sister's house in New York City. It was time to speak up.

I didn't waste a breath as I started in on all the things I'd been holding in for more than a decade. Initially, he tried to make excuses and rewrite history, but I shut him down, quickly.

"I have things I need to get off of my chest, and after all of these years, the least you can do is listen," I said, calmly.

I told him how I felt and how I'd been feeling, for years. Once I was done, I felt the heavy weight of the burdens from my early childhood instantly lift away from me. I was no longer angry or sad or resentful toward him. In fact, I felt like we could actually start building a new relationship. And just like that, my father was back in my life—plus a twenty-one-month-old sister, who reminded me of myself, and a nine-month-old brother, undeniably my father's son.

The two had been taken from my father's care because the Child Welfare Agency suspected he was addicted to crack. Once a week, my father and I would meet in front of the agency's office and, together, visit with my baby sister and brother. My sister seemed catatonic when we first entered the visiting room. But the instant her eyes found his, she'd light up, smiling and laughing, and fall under the spell of his charming-daddy ways. I completely understood how she felt. I had once been my daddy's little girl, too.

Those hour-long visits went on for weeks, until my father

started showing up late. He even missed one visit altogether. All this time, I'd been trying hard to deny that he might have a crack habit. But on another day, I caught a glimpse of him as I walked toward the building, and I was completely shocked by what I saw. He looked like walking death. He was terribly thin and just looked so sickly. I burst into tears and went on a rant about how much the babies needed him to get his life together.

That day, in the middle of that Bronx street, was the last time I saw or spoke to my father for the next five years.

During the time we were out of touch again, I realized that I'd made a terrible mistake in choosing a mate. By that time, my then-husband and I were living in Los Angeles. Slowly, my father began to resurface in my life. We talked on the phone occasionally, and he seemed to be in a better place after attending rehab and undergoing therapy. I was happy for him, but cautious about letting him get too close.

One day I heard the phone ring and then stop. Because my husband didn't say anything, I just assumed the call was for him. About thirty minutes later, he came into the living room and told me that my father was on the phone. I was stunned. My first thought was, *What news is he going to bring this time?* Then I thought, *Wait, what could he and my husband have been talking about for a half hour? They've never even met or spoken.*

When I picked up the phone, my father started berating me about how poorly I'd been treating my husband.

"I didn't raise you like that," he said.

I completely lost it!

"How dare you listen to what a man you don't even know tells you about your own daughter? If you want to know the truth, I never told you about what was going on in my life, or in my marriage, because I didn't want to worry *you*! And while you were talking to my husband for so long, did he tell you how he's been treating me?"

When I was done unloading, my father was silent for a few seconds. Then, in a slow, quiet, *angry* voice, he asked if I needed his protection. Something about his tone sent shivers through me.

"No, no. I'm handling it," I said, trying to sound convincing.

Though I was afraid for my husband—for a second—I was also kind of happy to have my father acting protective toward me. It softened my heart toward him once again. But it was also hard for me to ignore the role he had played in leading me into a volatile marriage in the first place.

After my parents divorced, my mother remarried when I was eleven. She'd met a man who always treated her like a queen. This gentle giant stepped right in to fill the void of my absent father, too. Not only was he deliberate about making a positive impact on my self-esteem and shaping my outlook on male-female relationships, he also demonstrated, daily, what a man should be and do for his family. He was the one who walked me down the aisle on my wedding day, too.

Unfortunately for me, my stepfather's efforts weren't strong enough to crack the foundation of what I'd already learned about interacting with men. That foundation had been laid down and built up by my father during my formative years. On numerous occasions, my father had admonished me to be nice and think of other people's feelings before mine. While that might seem like good parenting, in theory, I believe that his lessons morphed into a setup, making me susceptible to controlling men, many of whom used abusive tactics to manipulate me.

I remember hearing my father say to someone, "Cindy better not marry anybody like me!" The dynamic of our relationship eventually played out in all of my relationships, though, especially in my four-year marriage. My ex-husband had a manipulative nature, just like my father. While we were dating, he'd created a story about a cheating ex-girlfriend to gain my sympathy and loyalty. I remember how my father would never accept blame or responsibility for anything he did wrong. Instead, he insisted that my mother was always at fault. My ex-husband did just the opposite. If we had a problem, he'd give a full dissertation about how and why he was wrong and how and why he would change. I naively believed that his admissions meant he was capable of great communication, which I know to be the strong foundation for a solid relationship.

I was wrong about him.

My ex would invade my privacy constantly. He eavesdropped on my private conversations and stole my passwords so he could listen to my voicemails and read my emails. He also read my journals, including many that dated back to my childhood, and then used the information he'd read to ridicule and torment me. Gradually, he began to isolate me from close family and friends, too. Initially, I stayed in the marriage because I thought I could love him through it. I also kept hearing my father's voice . . .

Be nice. Think about other people's feelings.

By the time I realized I had to get out, my ex-husband's tactics had escalated and the relationship had gone from unhealthy to extremely dangerous. At one point, I was afraid to sleep in the same house with him. There were so many times when I wondered how I could have ended up in such a situation. I was fully aware of the horrors of domestic violence, but there I was, feeling scared and stuck.

After my father called me in Los Angeles that afternoon, I was in contact with him on an occasional basis. One year, he even sent me a birthday card, which was the first one I'd received from him since I was a little girl. Once I moved back to the East Coast, I would see him sometimes, usually in regard to my younger siblings. But over time, I started to notice a pattern. Whenever he called, there was always bad news. Sometimes, he'd complain that none of my siblings kept in touch with him, or about how someone else was treating him badly. When his birthday or Fathers Day rolled around, he'd try to make me feel guilty for not sending a card or gift. He was always sad or angry, and eventually it all became too much for my spirit. I dreaded seeing his name on my caller ID. Most of the time, I just didn't answer the phone when he called. If I chose to answer his calls, I tried to brace myself for the drama and negativity. My father always seemed to feel better after we spoke. I always felt worse.

As a grown woman, divorcée, and domestic violence survivor, I have suffered through my fair share of heartache, much of which I've attempted to combat with prayer, positive thinking, and advice from family and friends. Still, I knew that I needed to do more self-exploration. I needed to figure out how to disrupt the dysfunctional patterns in my life and break any generational curses at work. I asked God to show me the truth and give me answers about where I'd gone wrong. That's when I had a revelation about the parallels between my relationship with my father and my romantic relationships with men.

My father had not been consistently available, yet he would always seem very loving and caring when he was around. For most of my life, I realized, I'd been opening my heart to men who also were not fully available, whether emotionally or due to time or distance. Because I'd always believed that my father loved me despite his abuse, selfishness, and absence, I believed that other men who exhibited similar traits could love me, too. What I learned from my father was that I should make rationalizations when my needs were not being met. This, in turn, made me anxious. When my relationships could no longer bear the burden of doubt and unfulfilled expectations, I was left feeling frustrated and confused.

Once I had that revelation, I felt somewhat healed and had a better idea of what changes I needed to make in my life. I eventually ended a decade-plus, on-again, off-again relationship that,

I'm sure, had been blocking me from pursuing more fulfilling and healthy relationships. Since then, my faith in love and marriage have been renewed because I finally understand that it's not a question of whether to have hope, but rather where, and with whom, you choose to lay your hope.

It has been a few months since I last spoke to my father. A few years ago, I felt hopeful about a positive change in him. A few months after that, though, that glimmer of hope was quickly extinguished when I learned that he was involved in a violent incident with his current wife. It's always the same story.

I have forgiven him at different times, but I've found myself having to forgive him over and over again when faced with the hurtful realities his behavior has created. For my survival and continued healing and growth, I can no longer allow anyone to interact with me or those I love in that manner, not even my father. Having had my peace of mind stolen by him, first, and by my ex-husband, second, I don't ever want to feel that way again.

Because I'm not willing to compromise when it comes to living in peace, I have chosen not to speak with my father. That may change one day, but today is not that day. I love him. I feel for him. I want the best for him and I often wish that things could be better between us. I always want to know where he is and that he is okay, but for now, the best I can offer him is prayer and love—from a distance. ■

The Friendly Demon

KYRA GROVES

I LOVE MY FATHER. I am grateful for that. I am equally grateful that he didn't raise me. The three children of a woman he lived with for over fifteen years were not so lucky.

Hope has no home where the devil resides, and the devil resides within my father. I hate those words. I wish I could say they came to me from somewhere outside of my thoughts, but they didn't. Those words came directly from what I found out about his past. They came from the actions of a man who slowly and deliberately instilled self-loathing into three vibrant hearts. This man, my father, obliterated three children's spirits and squandered three innocent lives. He abused his role as their common-law parent and set each of them up to become lost, angry adults.

It's difficult for me to describe my father as the devil. I love him so much, but years ago, when I first learned about his role in that family, he seemed like nothing less than a monster. He still is, I suppose, but he's older and much more frail now, unable to inflict the same type of pain he once did. Alone, and well past his prime, he lives out his days oblivious to the harm he's caused. Or maybe he's in complete denial about it. I still don't know which. The one time I confronted him, he so vehemently denied everything that I walked away fueled further by anger. It was a year before I even spoke with him again, and several more before I found any peace and forgiveness.

Growing up, I had no clue that there was even anything to forgive. I didn't see the side of my dad that I now describe as the devil. If I did catch any hints or glimpses, they weren't obvious. Who I saw was the person everybody outside of that family saw—a kind, charming man, full of bravado and intellectual grace. *That* man was friendly and personable and well liked. He hosted cool neighborhood pool parties and camping trips to islands with big boulders to jump from. *That* man always told me I was wonderful and precious and "so very lovely made from love." In my world, Superman existed and he was none other than my dad.

What I got was the best of my father, and what he got was a kind, caring, well-balanced, and self-loving daughter. He got a daughter who has experienced loving and caring relationships—not without imperfections, of course, but certainly with an abundance of mutual respect, appreciation, and support. I'd like to thank my mother for that. It's not possible to talk about who I am—my journey, my choices, my father's influence on me, and his place in my heart—without mentioning my incredible mom.

My mother's role in parenting me was thoughtful, kind, and respectful of my father. Her choice to divorce him, when I was just a year old, was thoughtful, kind, and respectful of herself and of me. Leaving her marriage was the best thing she could have done for me, and the best way for her to allow my father to play a positive role in my life.

My mother, not yet aware of what my father was truly capable, always protected his character. He, on the other hand, always undermined hers. He would fill my head with trivial complaints and falsities whenever I'd visit him, and I would accuse my mom of cruel, unkind, and unjust behaviors the minute I got home. She never spoke a negative word about him, nor did she put up a defensive attack. Instead, she chose to focus her energy on providing me with love and getting us back to our daily routine. I needed nothing more than that. Within a few days, my raw feelings would subside, along with my memory of his complaints, and my mother's role remained safe and intact. Despite his careless tactics, she would allow his role to remain safe and integral to my life. More important, she made sure to incorporate many other people into my life as well. I grew up surrounded by amazing people.

There was her family, of course, which included my three insanely cool uncles, their outstanding wives, and my amazing grandparents, Dzia Dzi and Bobci. My mother's many friends, who came from all walks of life, added to the diversity of my thoughts, the strength of my opinions, and the eagerness of my spirit to be open and kind. We always knew our neighbors from the top of the block to the bottom, and the parents of my friends were never strangers in our home. My teachers and counselors were a part of our network, too, with an open line of communication established at the beginning of each school year. But another, unexpectedly salient set of people she made sure to introduce me to were the men in her life.

My mother didn't hide dating from me. Thank God for that. She was one beautiful, intelligent, witty, and classy woman—she still is—and she deserved to have good men in her life. She was working hard hours and raising a child on her own, so having a personal life offered her balance. Her relationships allowed me the opportunity to meet caring and adoring men who were as gracious and respectful of me as they were of her. I was shown trust and compromise in lieu of arguments and discord, and I absorbed different tiers of what I construed as love. My father, I might add, did not offer any of that to his ex and her children.

If this story was solely about my relationship with my dad, I might have shared all of the sordid details about what make him the devil by now. This story is not solely mine, though, and sharing the specifics would be considerably disrespectful. Just as my mother chose to protect me from details that served no purpose to my growth or understanding, I choose to protect the personal details of the others whom are entwined in this story. Only they can speak regarding the specifics of their experiences. I think that's only fair.

What I will say is that the things I learned about my father while he was with that family were bad. His abuse was tailored to each individual, and each of them was ultimately left with no real means to cope. He spent fifteen years injecting suspicion and discord into their home until there was no real sense of trust. He manipulated the perspectives through which other people viewed them, too, and diminished their characters. I, fortunately, went un-scathed by those tactics. I lived my childhood under my mother's care, blissfully believing he was a superhero. Having come to terms with who he is, I can now live my adulthood without the burden of his past. And while I am happy to have found peace within myself, I never disregard the sadness that comes from knowing how his actions damaged that family.

These days, I do not dwell on the anger or sadness. I no longer concern myself with whether my father thinks about his actions, or if he simply chooses to ignore all that he's done. And I no longer try to understand why others, cognizant of what was happening at the time, chose to ignore his abominable actions as well. I have no control over any of that. What I do have is a long-lost dream for those three children whom I'd always been so fond of. While it's much too late, I know, I quietly wish, with all of my heart, that their mother had made the same choices for them as my mother made for me. I wish she had left my father and spared herself and her precious children the pain they all endured. They deserved bet-ter and still do.

Maybe those are the lessons in all of this, if there are any. That you do your best to live your best, not only for yourself but also for those around you. That you strive to make decisions that sup-port your well-being, your spirit, and your heart. That you live life forgiving yourself and learning from the mistakes you make so as not to waste precious time, especially when children are involved. Once you take on the responsibility of a child, it's critical to look beyond yourself and get out of your own way where you might not have done so on your own. Children deserve a chance at a life that provides balance, stability, and support. They deserve a solid structure upon which to become strong, viable, balanced, and genuinely happy adults. They don't need to have two parents under the same roof for that to be achieved. In many cases, as in my own, it works out better if they don't.

What children need is someone who will protect and guide them until they can protect and guide themselves. My amazing mother did that for me. She taught me to make smart choices by making smart choices for herself. She taught me to love people for who they are, just how they are, and nothing less. She taught me to love myself because she loved herself, even if, initially, she found that love through me. It was through the good in her that I experienced the good in my dad. Compromising him would have compromised raising me. I only learned about the bad that existed in him *from* him—indirectly or directly, in my own time, when it was time—but never from my mom.

My mother is the reason why my father's early influence on me was a positive and healthy one. She's the reason why I've become a completely, imperfectly whole, decent, and sensitive human being. Her generous spirit has allowed me to walk with grace and a sense of responsibility for myself and for the others with whom I share my life. She's the reason why my mind and eyes remain open and why I wear a grateful smile and have little judgment or hate in my heart—unless there is mention of my apartment manager. That's a whole other essay, but hey, I'm ever-evolving, right?

I thank you, Mom, for the life you have given me and continue to enrich.

And I thank you, too, Dad, for the extraordinary parts you play, you friendly demon, you. May you never know this essay exists. ■

He Always Said, "I Love You"
TRESA L. SANDERS, AS TOLD TO THE EDITOR

FOR ME, IT'S ALL ABOUT THE STORY. I've always wanted to know the story, especially when it comes to my family. It doesn't matter how complicated the details are, either. I just want to know.

I was eighteen years old when I met my father. My parents split when I was two and as much as my mother *didn't* say about him when I was growing up, she never spoke ill of him. *Ever.* I knew he had to have a story, though. It took me a long time to piece it all together, but once I got to know him and learned where he came from, I was able to read his blueprint. I really understood what made him *him*. And I loved him.

The child who doesn't have a father usually creates one. That's exactly what I did. I was born and raised in Flint, Michigan, and most of the kids in my neighborhood and at school had their fathers at home, except for me and my siblings. I'm the youngest of my mother's six children and when I was five years old, I saw my three brothers dancing around the living room like James Brown. We always watched him on television, and when I realized that they could dance like him, I figured we must be related, right? I know it might sound crazy, but I started to imagine that the Godfather of Soul was my father.

Three years after I created a father, I got a huge surprise. I was visiting my maternal grandmother in Alabama over the summer, and my aunt took me and my cousin to see James Brown—*live*! Back in those days, and especially when he performed in the South, he'd have a stage built outside in an open field. He also made sure all of the kids came down to the front so he could interact with them. I was standing front and center at that show and I'll never forget the moment when he touched my little hand. At eight years old, that was the highlight of my young life, but by the time he left the stage, with his cape over his shoulders, my fantasy started to fade away. As much fun as it had been to imagine he was my father, I was getting old enough to know better. It was just a game I'd been playing with myself so I wouldn't feel so sad about not having my father at home. Eventually, I grew out of that phase.

I don't remember a time when my father lived with us. My mother, Johnnie, was eighteen when she married my father, Earnest Sanders. I believe he was twenty-eight then, but because his birth date didn't match on any of our birth certificates, I never knew his exact age. I did know that he'd already been married, twice, and had three other children. During their ten-year marriage, my mother had six children in eight years. They broke up for a while and my mother started dating another man and got pregnant. After my older sister, Sherry, was born and given my father's last name, my parents got back together, which is still so fascinating to me. Who *does* that? They had three more children together, including me, before their relationship ended for good.

My father moved to California, where he remained for my entire childhood. My mother moved on with her life, too. She reconnected with a man she knew from her younger days in Alabama, and I think she began living in a fantasy world of her own. She got caught up in the idea of rekindling an old flame, and a year before that James Brown concert, she got remarried. Unfortunately, my stepfather turned out to be an asshole. He was an alcoholic, too. What I remember most about him was that he was as mean as a rattlesnake, for no good reason.

Soon after they got married, we started moving around a lot. We lived in Alabama for less than a year and then moved to New York, where my mother had family, for two years. Then we moved back home to Flint. It was a stressful time for all six of us kids and I never understood why she put us through that. I still don't understand why she even married him, because she was doing fine raising us on her own. Even as a kid, I saw that my mother was someone who got shit done. She hadn't finished high school, but she sure knew how to work hard and hustle, which is why I'm a master at both. I watched her sell everything from CopperCraft and Home Interiors to Avon and clothes from a catalog. You name it, she could sell it, and *well*. We had three meals a day, every day, and beautiful clothes. We didn't have everything, but we definitely had what we needed. From my point of view, she was able to do it all and *was* doing it, but I can imagine that it wasn't always easy for her. But then, being married to my stepfather wasn't easy for her, either.

Life with my stepfather was pure turmoil. He had four children of his own, but it seemed that none of them wanted to have much to do with him. Ironically, they all adored my mother and seemed to prefer dealing with her. Along with having fractured relationships with his kids, he turned our house into an atmosphere full of yelling, tussling, and fighting, all fueled by his drinking. My mother has always been a tough cookie, and although she was able to handle herself, and him, I remember being so scared all of the time. Because I never really felt safe, I was always tiptoeing around and hiding in closets, just to stay out of the way. Until this day, whenever I watch a movie where a kid is running and ducking for cover, I see myself as a little girl and immediately tear up. That was my life. Thinking about those times still hurts.

The first time I can remember hearing my father's voice was when I was ten years old. He called once a year, at random, and would talk to all of us kids, one by one. Even though we didn't know what month, day, or time he would call again, we always looked forward to speaking to him. He'd never been around, but I knew, in theory, that on the other side of the phone was *my* father, and what mattered most was that he was so nice to me. Hearing his voice meant everything.

"I love you," he'd say.

He always said that.

Before I hung up or passed the phone on to one of my brothers or sisters, my father *always* said he loved me. That meant the world to me, and I believed him every time he said those three words. I needed to believe him because I was living in a house with a man who didn't love me. I don't think my stepfather loved anybody, but because my father told me he loved me, I felt loved. Those annual phone calls sustained me for years.

Then came the call *about* my father. These many years later, I can't remember who made that call, but I know it was somebody from his side. Some of my father's family lived in the same town, so he made sure we were connected to his brothers and our cousins. When we were growing up, my brothers, sisters, and I were really close with our cousins, but by this time, everybody was doing their own thing. As the baby of the family, I was the only one still in school and living at home with my mother, who'd finally left my stepfather when I was in eleventh grade. The following summer, between eleventh and twelfth grades, I was taking pre-college courses and one day, I walked in from school and heard the phone ringing. When I picked up, I was told that my father was in town and wanted to see me. I thought, *My father is here, in Flint . . . and he wants to see me? Oh my God!* The next day, he was at the house, waiting outside for me. It was just me and him.

There were a few pictures of him around the house, in old photo albums, so I had an idea about what he looked like. Seeing his face, in the flesh, was a completely different experience. He was a handsome man, and as I took a closer look at him, I saw so much of my brother, Billy. He looked like my sister, Selina, too. I also noticed his dimples, which started as deep creases in the middle of his cheeks and ran down to his jawline, just like mine. Even before he hugged and kissed me and told me he loved me, I was in awe. Oh, and he was just so nice, just like I'd imagined he would be. I was super happy, and I believed him when he said he was coming back to see me the next day. When I got to school that next morning, I couldn't contain myself.

"Guess what? My father came to see me yesterday," I said to anybody who would listen. "I'd never met him and it was so great to see him. Yesterday was the best day of my life!"

I didn't know that he wouldn't come back that next day like he said he would, but I wasn't upset. I was fine, actually. I think I'd already accepted the fact that he was like a ship passing in the night, and in my mind, he'd just floated back to wherever he'd been before. I didn't know why he was in town or why he didn't show up the next day, but because all I'd ever wanted was to meet him, I didn't have any expectations. My life went on.

When I was twenty-two, I found out I was pregnant. The plan was to move to Los Angeles with my boyfriend, get married, and start a new life together. I remember hoping that our marriage would be forever because I didn't want to get divorced like my parents. After growing up without my father and enduring such madness with my stepfather, I knew that I wanted to be with someone who could take care of me, but not in the monetary sense. I needed to feel like I was protected, which is something I never had. I'm still looking for that today, unfortunately. Back then, I didn't realize just how much my upbringing had affected my outlook on life and relationships.

To be honest with myself, and fair to my ex-boyfriend, our relationship ended because I overreacted about a situation that, in hindsight, was not a deal-breaker. The night before we were supposed to go down to the justice of the peace, I got mad at him for hanging out with his friends. I didn't understand the concept of a bachelor party, so I thought he was being irresponsible. When I found out he was drinking, too, I flashed back to the horrors of my childhood and convinced myself that he would become a raging alcoholic like my stepfather. I thought social drinking or getting drunk, even one time, was an early sign of addiction, and I didn't want any part of it. Despite being young and very pregnant, I called everything off that night. Being a single mother hadn't been part of my plan, but I was more terrified about the possibility of reliving the past. My knee-jerk decision wasn't about my boyfriend, though. I knew it was all of my stuff, but I still couldn't go through with it. I just couldn't marry him.

Just like in The Whispers song "Olivia," I found myself living in Los Angeles and feeling very "lost and turned out." I was lost, for sure, but unlike the lyrics to that song, I thought I might end up *sleeping* on the streets rather than working them. Right after my son was born, I was damn-near homeless until I found a room-mate—someone I met, by chance, in a convenience store. She and I got along well, but her boyfriend wasn't quite right. He suffered from post-traumatic stress after serving in the military and would have outbursts that scared the hell out of me. When I found him in the parking lot one night, shouting orders to people who weren't there, I knew I had to get myself and my baby out of that environment. I guess word spread back home that I was having a tough time on the West Coast because, out of the blue, I got a call from my cousin Willie, from my father's side.

"You know your father is in LA, right?" Willie asked me. "I told him you were out there and he wants you to call him. Here's his number."

As I reached for a pen, I thought it was strange that I'd not even thought about my father during my time in Los Angeles. I was the same girl who'd been so excited about meeting him a few years earlier, yet he hadn't even crossed my mind, and we were in the same state, in the same city. I was really in a tough spot, so I called him up. I had nothing to lose.

"What's going on?" he asked. "What are you doing?"

When I told him the crazy tale about my roommate's boyfriend, he said I could stay with him.

"Okay, I'm coming," I said. "I'm on my way."

I packed up my stuff, grabbed my little boy, and drove over to my father's house. I had not seen him since that summer when I was eighteen, and now we were going to be sharing a two-bedroom apartment. Life is a trip.

"Don't worry about paying me rent," he said when I arrived. "You don't have pay for electricity or anything else. I just want you to get on your feet."

I looked at him and busted out laughing.

"Oh, I know I wasn't going to pay any rent because you didn't pay any child support," I said. "You owe me, my brothers, and my sisters child support, so you don't have to worry about me paying for *nothing*!"

He just laughed. He thought I was the funniest person in the world. In that moment, I was laughing, too, but I was serious. Over time, I noticed that whenever the subject of child support came up, he'd get really quiet. I think he knew that he hadn't been a good father or husband and just didn't want to talk about it.

As I'd gotten older, I would ask questions about my father and my mother started speaking up. She told me about the early days, when he owned a record store, which he lost because he mismanaged his money. And aside from never providing her with any financial support, there was another issue in their relationship that I found more shocking—my father was still legally married to someone else when he met my mother. Rather than filing the necessary paperwork to get divorced between marriages, he just moved on. When he married my mother and created our family, he was technically still married to his previous wife, which meant that my mother wasn't able to divorce him and had to annul their union. What a mess. Hearing that story was very upsetting, but I also wondered if maybe it was a sign of the times. I doubt that my father was the first person during that time who failed to handle his personal affairs, but then again, the whole situation spoke to his irresponsibility as a man.

I learned so much about him during that year we lived together. For one, my father, whom everybody in Los Angeles called "Sandy," was not capable of taking care of himself. He worked as a presser at a family-owned dry cleaner, but I noticed that he never had much cash on him. I never saw him writing any checks, either, so instead of trying to guess how he was handling his money, I just asked him. He told me, straight-up, that his boss held onto his checks and paid his bills for him. The little pocket change I'd seen him with was basically an allowance to make sure he had a few dollars on him, just in case. His boss did that because he cared about my father and his well-being. It seemed that everybody picked up the slack for him because he couldn't do it for himself.

I also noticed that he drank too much. My father was a nice, lovable man, and even though his demeanor was nothing like my stepfather's, he was every bit an alcoholic. Not that I wanted to, but I knew how to deal with someone who was addicted to alcohol. When I realized that my father was doing drugs, too, I knew I had to go. I didn't want to live like that, not with my son. Actually, my son, who was just learning to walk at the time, tipped me off. He'd be crawling and walking all around the apartment, and I'd find him holding things in his hands or in his mouth that I didn't recognize. I remember seeing him play with a long, glass tube, and when I bent down to take it away from him, I thought, *What is that? Is that a pipe?*

I was rushing out to work one morning when I realized I'd forgotten my keys. When I walked back into the apartment, I saw my father leaning against the doorway of his room, facing inside. He didn't flinch when I walked in, nor did he make a move when the front door closed behind me. As I got closer to him, I noticed him taking a long drag off of a pipe like the one my son had found on the carpet. *Oh my God, my father smokes crack*, I thought to myself as I walked toward my bedroom. He still didn't move a muscle. He didn't move when I walked past him again, nor did he move when I walked out of the apartment. By the time I made it out to the car, my mind was made up. I had already been thinking about going back to Flint because I wasn't making enough money to live on my own in Los Angeles, but after what I'd seen, I knew it was time to go. But first, I wanted to talk to my father about his substance abuse.

"So, you smoke crack?" I asked him when I got home from work that day.

He looked at me and responded with, "What are you talking about?"

"I saw you smoking crack," I said. "I stood right here this morning and *saw* you smoking crack."

"Your eyes are lying to you, Tresa," he said. "You didn't see nothin'."

My father didn't even blink when he spoke to me. Those words just slipped off of his tongue, which was a blow, and also a lesson. In that instant, I knew how easily a man could look you dead in your face and lie. I felt for him because he was clearly very troubled, but I'll never forget that exchange. I tried not to take it personally because it was only a part of the time we'd spent together. But still, it was time for me to leave, so that's what I did.

Despite ending on such a disappointing note, the year I spent with my father was actually a good experience for me. I'd set out to learn more about him, and that's exactly what I got. I got to know him and see his spirit. He got to know me, too, and I think there were parts of me that reminded him of himself. Even though I didn't grow up with him in my life, it was great to see him be a grandfather to my son. He just loved spending time with his grandson.

After leaving Los Angeles to return to Flint, I later moved to New York, where my son grew into a young man, and still later, I relocated to Atlanta. Work required me to be on the road a lot, but no matter what city I was living in or traveling to, I was always in touch with my father. He was my homie. He was charming and funny and had a great personality, so I understood why people wanted to be in his company. I could see why my mother had fallen in love with him—and also why she had to leave him, even with six kids. I respected her so much for not telling me about his issues because I was glad to have discovered them on my own, as an adult.

The fantasy I'd had about him being with me when I was a kid was just that—a fantasy. In reality, he was completely irresponsible and could have never been a father to me or any of my siblings. He wasn't there for us, physically, but he is very much a part of us. The only one of my siblings I haven't met yet is my oldest brother, from my father's first marriage, but when I met my brother Kenneth, from his second marriage, he had the same cool demeanor as Billy, who was just like my father. As for me, I'd say that my slick mouth is what I got from him. I can talk shit when I feel like it, and that was all him. In my eyes, he was forever young, which is how I've always felt about myself, too. I definitely got that from him.

My father moved back to Flint and was on his own for a while before he was afflicted with dementia. When he was no longer able to live by himself, we all stepped up. My cousin Debra was even able to care for him around the clock. It was ironic, having to be responsible for someone who had never been responsible for himself or his family, but that's what it was and you do what you have to do. I took care of things from afar, financially, and called and visited as often as I could. Whenever I was in town, I'd spend time with him. Sometimes, I'd just take him out to the store to make sure he had what he needed, whether it was underwear or socks or whatever else. I did my best to make sure he was covered. He was my father.

As his illness progressed, there were times when he didn't recognize anybody, but he always knew who I was when I walked through the door. And on occasions when he became difficult to deal with, I would just say, "Stop," and he would calm down. People would tell me how different he seemed when I was around, and I knew why. Our relationship was solidified after we shared that two-bedroom apartment. I felt bad, though, about being the only one of his children, besides Kenneth, whom he'd ever really bonded with. We'd all missed out when we were kids, and because of that, not all of my siblings felt about him the way I did. My heart still breaks when I think about how my late sister Tina, from his second marriage, used to talk about the early years of her life, when he was there.

"I was Daddy's little girl," she'd say as she cried. "He just loved me so much."

As far as I know, he never apologized to any of his children. While I was able to forgive him, I also understand that everybody has a different walk. And like Tina, who passed away in her late fifties, a few of my brothers and other sisters weren't able to move beyond the pain. That makes me sad, but I respect how they feel. It was never a good situation, for any of us.

After we buried him, I had a long conversation with my aunt, his sister, who really opened my eyes about who my father was *before* he became my father. She said that all of her brothers had problems with alcohol, which is something I hadn't known. She also told me things that he never shared—mainly the fact that his mother died when he was two and he never knew his father. I was stunned. He was a motherless *and* fatherless child, which is something I cannot imagine. He had to have felt an extreme amount of displacement as a child, and since he didn't grow up with parents, how would he know how to be one? I don't excuse him for not being responsible, but I understand why he wasn't able to be the man I wanted him to be. Perhaps he wanted to do things differently, too, but just didn't know where to start. As hard as it is to admit, I think it was probably better that he wasn't a part of my day-to-day life when I was growing up.

My father wasn't perfect, but I've learned that sometimes you have to look beyond a person's issues and accept them for who they are, *where* they are. I accepted my father as he was. I loved him and I know he loved me the best way he could, even when he wasn't there.

As much as I miss him now, I'm thankful to have learned his story. Finally, I know the story. ∎

All Is Forgiven

CORI MURRAY

I wouldn't say that I hated my father, but there was definitely a time when I couldn't have cared less if he was in my life. At least that's the lie I used to tell myself.

I was on a business trip when my mom called to tell me that he'd died. As much as the news saddened me, I wasn't really surprised. I'd been expecting that call for many years, ever since he chose drugs over being a present father to me and my brother— well, actually, that would be *brothers*, plural.

But I'm getting ahead of myself.

For so long, I felt as though my father had let go of the rope we'd both been holding onto. I assumed that he didn't want to hang on anymore, that he was just . . . done. His death certificate states that he died due to complications from diabetes mellitus, but really, his passing had more to do with his broken soul. I'd always believed that he didn't care about me and my younger brother, Ian, but that wasn't the case. When I asked my mom why he didn't try hard enough for us, she gave me an answer that she'd already accepted for herself.

"Your father loved you both, with all he had, but he just didn't have enough for himself," she said.

Her words were like a revelation. As I wiped away my tears, I knew that I'd have to find it in my heart to forgive the sins I'd been holding against him. He'd been carrying around enough extra baggage. I had, too.

You see, when my dad died, I felt like I'd been cheated. After he and my mother divorced, it seemed like he just skated away, clean, without having to make up for the years he was in and out of my life. When I see the kind of father my daughter is blessed to have—attentive, loving, playful, compassionate, responsible, caring—I understand what a difference it makes for a girl to have her dad there, physically and emotionally. I realize just how much I didn't get.

Now, Momma likes to say that my dad loved me. She also tells me that he was around, but I don't have any memories of him from before I was in third grade—not any good ones, anyway. Ian and I were always close to his family, so we knew he was proud that we were his kids. Even though he wasn't with us for many years, it's not like we didn't know who he was or where he came from. We knew. But I, for one, didn't have any warm and fuzzy thoughts about him. And there's one incident that I'll never forget.

When I was about seven years old, my parents were arguing and my father hit my mother in the head with a cast-iron skillet. I overheard the commotion through the walls of the bedroom that Ian and I shared at Big Momma's house. What my father didn't know was that my grandmother kept a small pearl-handled gun under her bed. In no time, she'd grabbed her weapon and was standing between them. She told my father to leave before she shot him. I don't doubt that she would have.

I snuck out of the bedroom and saw my father just standing there, fuming. He'd been defeated by an old woman. He started to walk away, but then he turned around and said that we were all going to hell.

"Well, nigga, we'll meet you there!" Big Momma seethed, still pointing her gun in his direction.

After that night, I didn't see my dad for four years. He was in the Air Force and had received an assignment in Japan. While he was gone, my mother got remarried to a man I barely remember. We even moved to Chicago with her new husband, who wanted us to call him "daddy," which was hard for me. Although he hadn't been around, I was very clear that I already *had* a daddy.

Six months after the wedding, we all moved back to Texas, and within a few more months, my mom, Ian, and I were back where we started—living with Big Momma. Until this day, I still don't know why Momma's second marriage ended. I still don't care enough to even ask. What did concern me was the fact that my father would soon be back in our lives. One day, my mother said casually, "Your dad is on his way over here."

The image I had of him in my mind was blurry, but as I peeked through the blinds and saw him walking across the front yard, I thought, *Yeah, that's him.* I had butterflies in my stomach. I wanted to jump into his arms when he walked through the front door. I wanted to yell, "Boy, where you been?"

"Hello," I said instead, politely.

Then we gave each other an awkward hug. Come to think of it, that's exactly how we'd be in each other's company for years to come—pleasant and kind of awkward. After we greeted each other, he handed me the gift he was holding in his hands. I looked down at the Casio recorder and smiled, immediately forgetting all of the years he'd been gone.

My parents were married right after high school and got divorced four years later. Unbeknownst to me and Ian, who is two years younger, they were now trying to rekindle their young love. Plans were also in motion for us to go live with him—but not *just* him. We were going to be living with his first child, our new, three-years-older-than-me brother, William, whom Ian and I had never met and didn't even know existed. There was even more news. We were moving to Washington, DC. My dad was to be stationed at Andrews Air Force Base and we'd all be living under one roof.

Oh, and did I mention that the five of us would be driving there, *together*, for twenty-plus hours?

So, here are the highlights of the first two years of my new life with Daddy. "Washington, DC" turned out to be Suitland, Maryland, a gritty, blink-and-you'll-miss-it suburb fifteen minutes outside of the nation's capital. At my new school, I was teased for having long hair, a country accent, and wearing penny loafers. One of my fondest memories from those days is the night we all sat in the living room, as a family, and watched Michael Jackson do the moonwalk for the first time on the Motown 25 TV special. I also remember when Ian and I discovered that William was into heavy metal. We'd stare at him in utter amazement as he rocked out to Ozzy Osbourne and Black Sabbath. That was definitely new.

We'd visited the Smithsonian and other historical landmarks during our first summer weekends, but after we started school, we didn't really do too much outside of the house. I remember hearing my mother trying to encourage my father to provide us kids with things other than shelter and food. Instead of hugs and kisses, Daddy bought us dinner. Instead of taking us to the movies, he made sure the gas tank was full. She wanted him to spend time with us and expose us to different experiences, whether it be a trip to the mall or just a Sunday drive through Rock Creek Park. For some reason, he didn't seem capable of doing those things once we got settled.

I soon came to see just how disconnected he was from us, and *me*. Once, my mother asked him to pick up a few things for me from the store. I'm not sure what she told him that I needed, specifically, but he felt that the equivalent was a three-pack of underwear. As he handed me the package, I felt like a kid whose loving father was giving her the toy of her dreams. *What could be in the bag?* When I realized that he was handing me pink and white floral panties, in a size 4–6, my giddiness quickly faded. I looked up, meeting his eyes, and I saw the proud grin on his face turn to confusion.

"What's wrong?" he asked. "Your momma said you needed some underwear."

"Yeah, but Dad, I wear a 10. The size you bought could fit my doll," I said.

"Well . . . " was all he said. Then he walked off.

He just left me there, holding the underwear and wondering. *Not only does my dad not know what size I wear, but he also thinks I'm six years old.* I was mad at him and embarrassed *for* him. Had he not seen me every day for the last few months? Did he not look at me and think, *Wow, my little girl is growing up*? As the mother of a seven-year-old, I notice when my daughter has grown a half inch overnight. How could my own father not know me, not *see* me? But I wasn't the only one he had a problem connecting with.

The good intentions he had to bond with William were quickly unraveling. They just did not click. By our second year together, their relationship went from stable to rocky to volcanic, and it became increasingly uncomfortable to be in the house with them. To spare her own son from Daddy's abusive wrath, Momma started making arrangements for both Ian and me to live with her brother in Los Angeles. When we left Daddy and his firstborn behind, they believed that we were going to visit Momma's family for spring break. They had no idea of our ulterior motives.

Once Ian and I got to Texas, we stomped around our old neighborhood for a week or so, then we went into hiding at the home of one of Big Momma's friends. For two weeks, we stayed inside of that hot house and watched as my grandmother's friend ate Vienna sausages and crackers, every single day. Once my dad and his family figured out that we were "missing," intentionally, and stopped threatening my mom for taking "Murray's kids," we boarded a flight to Los Angeles. Ian didn't seem to know what was going on, but I did. When I broke the news that we weren't going back to Daddy, he cried.

The best year and a half of my childhood was spent away from my father. Bidding farewell to cold, dreary East Coast winters was an added bonus. I was officially a teenager living in Southern California, where it was summer every day! I felt like Sally Field in *Gidget*. I went to a junior high that was bigger than any school I'd ever seen in my life. I kissed a boy. I wore Bongo jeans and Wet *n* Wild lipstick. I shaved my legs. I went to the mall with my friends. I read *Seventeen*, *Right On!*, and *Teen Beat* magazines. I really felt like my future was so bright, but unfortunately, my mother, who'd been there to greet us when we arrived in Los Angeles, was having a really tough time with getting everything in place.

My uncle gave us a car and even though it was a total piece of shit, it was better than the nothing we'd arrived with. We did some couch-surfing, too, before we found an apartment—a one-bedroom—of our own. I remember that we couldn't invite anybody over because there wasn't any food to spare. Later, we got evicted when my mom lost her job. Then we moved in with my dad's sister's family, who lived nearby, while my mother tried to figure out her next move.

As much as I didn't want to leave California, I could see that she didn't have many choices. Going back to Texas to live in her mother's house, with two growing kids, was a fate worse than death. So, we went back to Maryland, to my dad. The three of us walked into our old apartment with our heads hung low. None of us wanted to be back there.

Initially, I wasn't sure what my father had been doing during the time we were gone. Ian and I hadn't really communicated with him while we were in California, and to be honest, I didn't miss not knowing what was happening in his life. It didn't take very long to see exactly what was going on, though.

The apartment was shrouded in darkness as a result of my father's growing drug habit. Now there was something else to deal with. There were times when we thought the apartment had been robbed, but after he'd start tripping over his own lies, it was obvious who the culprit was. Then there were those nights when we thought he was working a double shift but later found out he'd been out getting high with his buddies. Other than weed, I'd never seen my father do drugs, but when he started smoking crack, the physical effects were hard to miss.

"Your daddy was a good-looking man," Big Momma used to tell me.

Not anymore. He started to look haggard. He was losing his teeth, and his eyes were sullen, too. Once a portly man, he had withered down to the point where his clothes draped on him.

On most days, my father was a decent man. If there was something we needed, and if he was sober, he'd be like any other normal dad. And sometimes, dads just don't get it. When I was in eighth grade, I got my period, but I didn't have any pads. It was just me and him at home that day, and it took what felt like hours for me to figure out how to tell him. Although I'd clearly fumbled the entire situation, he read my body language, rolled his eyes with a smile, and took me to the store. I was hoping he'd take me to the commissary on the base, a place where I knew I wouldn't see anybody from my middle school. Instead, he headed for the 7-Eleven up the block where everybody hung out. I begged him to go inside and buy the pads for me, but he refused and starting yapping about how it was no big deal.

"It's a natural thing, Cori," he insisted.

When I walked into the store, I saw some kids from school, just as I'd feared. I was horrified. The entire purchase seemed to happen in slow motion. I just wanted to disappear, even after I slunk back into the car with the paper bag tucked under my arm.

"See, that wasn't so bad, right?" my father asked.

I almost died of embarrassment that day, but I can laugh about the experience now. Ever since then, I don't care who sees me walking down the "feminine care" aisle.

Thanks to Ian, we had some moments of joy at home. He was the court jester in the family and no matter what was going on, he always knew how to make Momma laugh. I remember the time when he pretended my nose was a vacuum cleaner that was sucking him up with each breath I took. Minutes before he rammed his bony, twelve-year-old body into my face, my mother was sulking about something my father had done, or didn't do. But once Ian starting making sucking noises and sticking his head up under my nose, my mother looked over at us.

"Let me *go*, Cori!" he screamed.

Because she'd been so deep in thought, in her own world, she was a little late on the joke. When she could no longer ignore his antics, she fell off of the sofa, howling with laughter. I hadn't seen her laugh like that in years.

High school was a time when I was completely focused on myself. I was hell-bent on doing everything I could to get into college. That was my primary focus. I'd joined Future Business Leaders of America, the Student Government Association, and even ROTC. I was on the softball team and the pom-pom squad, and I'd signed up to be a Maryland State Assembly page, too. My dream had been to attend New York University or Spelman College, but wait lists and tuition costs kept those schools beyond my reach. Life had something else in store for me, though. I found that Hampton University offered me the best deal, and the campus was just a three-hour drive from home. I happily accepted. I was excited.

Before I was to leave for college, life became turbulent, both inside and outside of our home. Nearly ten boys from my high school and neighborhood had been shot and killed over drugs. Meanwhile my father's habit had become even more of a regular routine. William had gone to live with his mother and Ian, once my little brother, was starting to tower over all of us. He wasn't so little anymore, and as he matured into a young man, he lost more respect for Daddy with each passing day. Their relationship deteriorated to nearly nothing, and one afternoon, their fighting became so physical that my friend and I had to step between them. It was a rough time.

My mother was working two jobs to support our household then. I was working, too, but she let me keep my money for nineteen-year-old essentials like clothes, lipstick, hair gel, and of course, cassette tapes. All the while, notices about my tuition were coming in from Hampton, but she assured me that everything would be worked out. I don't know how she managed, but she did, and I continued buying supplies for my future dorm room. I couldn't wait to get to college, but on the night before I was scheduled to leave, I was a nervous wreck. My feelings were bittersweet, I knew, but they were also compounded with anxiety because my father had not come home.

He'd left work hours before, but still hadn't walked through the door. By morning, I was done packing and started loading up the car. Ian, Momma, and Big Momma, who'd flown up from Texas to join us for my college drop-off, were all up too, helping me get all of my stuff together. My father still wasn't home. Once everything and everybody was in the car, I stood outside for a minute, looking, *waiting*, for him to show up. *Where was he?*

For most of that morning, my mom had been the quiet, patient mother she's always been. But once she saw me just standing there, she stepped out of herself and shook me out of my delusion. My father was not coming.

"Cori, get in the car," she said firmly. "Let's go."

I heard her. Then, as I fought back tears, I got behind the wheel, turned on the car, and drove off.

Years later, after several visits to a therapist, I retold that story. In my mind, the memory had been shaped into just another day that my dad disappointed me, but my therapist's reaction was so emotional, I felt like I needed to console *her*. She told me I'd been deeply damaged by that experience. She said that my father not showing up that day—which was something I hadn't spoken of since the day it happened—made me believe I wasn't good enough or wanted.

As she said the words out loud, I couldn't stop the tears that followed. I went right back to that day when I had been standing on that sidewalk, waiting for him to come home. I hadn't thought my relationship with my father had any effect on how I was living my life, but the evidence was there: I had a shitload of insecurities, I was dating mediocre men, and my self-esteem was tied to outside validation rather than internal motivation. What kept me from spiraling further was my mom's devotion to my going further than she had. Her love was big enough to keep me and Ian from feeling lopsided. She made us whole.

For many years after that, I kept contact with my father to a minimum. Since he'd missed most of the major moments in my life—from my college graduation to my big move to New York—I figured there was no need to keep regular tabs on him. I spoke frequently with Big Daddy, my paternal grandfather, who would update me on what was going on with my dad, who'd moved back to Texas. If he was there when I spoke to my grandfather, we might talk for a few minutes. I'd try to condense a year's worth of my life into a six-minute sound bite. Other than that, our interactions were limited to quick conversations on Christmas, Thanksgiving, and birthdays—*his*, not mine. When Fathers Day rolled around, I could count on my mother, Big Momma, or my great-aunt Claudene to hit me with the same line . . .

"He's still your father."

Some years, I'd call him on Fathers Day. Other years, I didn't. Then one year, after not hearing from him for months, he called me on my new cell phone. This was when cell phones were primarily used for emergencies, so my first thought was that something might be wrong. *Was he in the hospital? Was Big Daddy okay?* Then, for a fleeting moment, I hoped that he was calling to catch up. Did he want to start a dialogue with *me*? Maybe.

First, I noted the shallowness in his voice. Then I heard shame. My father wanted money. As he begged me to wire him $500, I wanted to scream. I was in shock. I wanted to throw the phone against the wall, as if shattering it would shatter *him*, too. But instead of giving into my rage, I told him that he'd broken my heart by not caring about me. I told him how much it hurt me that he could let my birthday pass, year after year, yet he could pick up the phone to ask for drug money. He was quiet. I couldn't tell if he was crying, silently, but I knew he was listening, because he never asked me for money again.

For the first few years after I finished college, it was obvious when I saw my father that the drugs still had a strong hold on him. I remember during one visit, I could barely look at him. We both turned away from each other, not knowing what to say. Then I started noticing a change. Because we didn't speak very often, it was from other family members that I learned he'd gotten a job as a short-order cook. He didn't have a car, so he was walking the two miles to and from work. I also learned that he'd been diagnosed with diabetes and was in and out of the hospital for treatments. All the while, he had a woman in his life. Overall, things seemed kind of stable. I'd see him a few times when I was in town to visit Big Momma, and he looked like the dad I remembered all those years ago in Maryland. Eventually he met my daughter, his third granddaughter, for the first time, too. We talked and laughed a little bit during those short visits, but there still weren't any warm embraces. Our smiles were genuine, though.

A few years ago, my former assistant was getting married in Texas, so I thought I'd fit a little family reunion into my trip, too. I'd been hearing that diabetes had started to get the best of my father. Part of his foot had been amputated and he'd also become insulin dependent. I hadn't seen him since his surgery.

My little girl traveled with me, and after the wedding festivities, we went to visit my dad. The three of us traipsed all over Fort Worth, visiting folks and eating at Ruby's and Whataburger. While were having lunch one day, I watched as he talked and played with his granddaughter, and she just laughed and played along with him. Right then, some of the lingering resentment and past hurt began to melt away. I wondered if maybe he could love her enough to make up for all of the time he hadn't been able to be my father. Then the moment passed.

My father died on December 12, 2013, three months after our last visit. At his funeral, I thought our years of estrangement would keep me from memorializing him with a full heart, but that wasn't the case. I thought about what my mother had said to me on the day she called to tell me that he died. Despite the choices he'd made, he *did* love me. He loved us and we loved him, too. That's really what mattered.

After the service, I took a deep breath and felt my spirit lift a bit. With tears in my eyes, I looked up and felt as though all was forgiven. It was . . . and it is. ■

Every Time You Go Away

ALYSSE ELHAGE

O NE OF THE EARLIEST MEMORIES I HAVE of being with both of my parents is an afternoon we spent together at a nature park when I was about four years old. I remember skipping alongside them as they held hands and smiled at each other, which is something I'd never seen them do before. That memory is so special to me because even though they were divorced at the time, there was a feeling of reconciliation in the air. We even stopped to have a family photo taken that was ironed onto a T-shirt.

Their divorce had been finalized for two years by that point, but I was still having trouble adjusting, especially when it came to going back and forth between their two households. There were those times when I couldn't go to sleep at my father's house unless my mom came over to tuck me in, and when I'd have an emotional meltdown as he dropped me off at her house after a visit. But that day at the park, I experienced what it was like for us to be a complete family, and I felt so happy and whole. Unfortunately, that feeling did not last very long.

Not only did my parents not reconcile, but a short time after that outing, my father broke the news that he was getting married again—to someone else.

"Don't you love Mommy anymore?" I asked him.

"I will always love your mother," he said.

Although his answer confused me, for many years I used his words to convince myself that my parents still loved each other. Believing that myth was easier than wondering if maybe they shouldn't have been together in the first place because, well . . . where would that leave me?

In many ways, my parents' marriage was a failed attempt to unite two very different cultures. They met in college and dated for about six months before getting married. My father was a handsome Lebanese immigrant with a charming smile who wrote my mom the most beautiful love poems. My mom, then an all-American beach girl, had fallen head over heels for the romantic young man who reminded her of Omar Sharif. A few months after they wed, my father whisked her off to Lebanon to meet his large, Catholic family, who welcomed her with open arms. She fell in love with them right away, along with Lebanon's cosmopolitan culture and generous people. After spending two weeks together in his homeland, it wasn't hard for my father to convince her to move back with him one day.

After returning to the States, their honeymoon phase quickly deteriorated into a web of newlywed struggles that were magnified by their cultural differences. When my mother discovered she was pregnant, I think they both hoped that having a child would be a kind of second chance. They named me after my paternal grandmother, and when I was six months old, we moved to Lebanon to start our new life. But things did not go the way my parents had hoped.

We arrived at the beginning of what became a nearly twenty-year-long civil war, which tore the country apart and, eventually, unraveled my parents' marriage. We were trapped in Lebanon for a year and spent a lot of that time crouched in the closet of my grandparents' mountain home during bombings. In the midst of all the unrest, I was also surrounded by most of my extended family in that tiny village, where I celebrated my first birthday, took my first steps, and said my first word, "baba," which is Arabic for "dad." As the war dragged on, the tension between my parents escalated. My father wanted to stay, but my mother wanted to leave, and by the time she was finally able to convince him that it was time to go, their marriage was basically over. Not long after we landed back on US soil, my mom filed for divorce.

Although I was very young when they split, the end of my parents' marriage was devastating for me because it meant that my father would never live at home with us again. While my mom got full custody, my father's presence in my life was reduced to weekend and summer visits, and a monthly check. At a time when I wanted and needed so much from him, I went from having his full attention and support to getting bits and pieces of his time. Gradually, I lost first place in his life, which is something I've never really gotten over.

While we rarely seemed to have enough time together, he always did his best to make the most of our visits. One of our favorite things to do was take long bike rides down to the river park near his house. My father would sit me in front of him on his bike and instruct me to keep my feet away from the wheel. I remember leaning back against him, breathing in his special scent of pine trees and lemon, and feeling ridiculously happy. At the park, we'd fish together and walk along the concrete wall around the river. On one of our last visits to that park, he used his pocketknife to carve the words, "Baba Loves Alysse," into an old tree near the riverbank. That's a moment I'll always cherish.

During our six weeks of summer, we'd drive twelve hours from Florida to Kentucky, where we'd spend two weeks with my aunt, uncle, and cousins. My grandparents often visited during that time too. I'd eat my aunt's spicy Lebanese dishes and play with my cousins for hours before falling asleep to the oddly comforting sounds of the adults "shouting" at each other in Arabic.

As much as I enjoyed visiting his side of the family, my favorite event of every summer was our "date night." My father and I would get dressed up and go to Red Lobster, where we ate seafood platters and I sipped on Shirley Temples. At dinner, we'd talk about what was going on in my life, at home and at school. Sometimes, I'd try to tell him how much I wanted to spend more time with him, but he would often interrupt me before I could finish.

"I know, but what can I do?" he'd say. "I have other responsibilities now."

For as long as I can remember, my stepmother was a part of my father's life—first as his girlfriend and later as his wife. Once they were married, I started feeling as though I had to share him with her, instead of the other way around. While she has always been kind to me, our relationship is complicated. In some ways, I think she viewed me as a part of my father's past that she wished he could forget. I think she also felt that my presence was an intrusion on the new life they were trying to build together, which meant that I did not always feel welcome. Once my brother and sisters were born, everything really shifted. My father tried to make me feel like a part of his new family, but I increasingly felt like an outsider as I watched him be the full-time father to my siblings that he could not be to me. As much as I loved my siblings, it was really hard for me to share what little time I had with my father with anyone else—including them.

While I tried to adjust to the changes at my father's house, life with my mom was in flux as well. We were generally happy, but our life was often chaotic and unstable. Even though she worked hard to support us, she struggled to make ends meet. There was also the matter of the series of men she brought in and out of our lives. By the time I started first grade, she was on her third marriage—to her high school sweetheart, a bearded man with a bad temper. Although he never hit us, my stepdad was verbally abusive, and I feared him. My mom, however, didn't seem to see his bad side. She believed that she'd found her "lost love" and bent over backwards to make the marriage work, including asking me to call him "daddy," which is a word I came to hate.

When I was eight, my mom gave birth to my sister and we moved to a beach town six hours away, where she and my stepdad started a new business. The move meant that I rarely had those special weekends with my father. I don't know if it was because I was missing him so much, but I started drawing closer to God during that time. My mother once told me that she "gave me to Jesus" before I was born, so I always felt that I had a special connection to the Lord. I'd also fallen in love with Amy Grant's song, "Father's Eyes," and I remember being surprised to learn that the lyrics were about God and not her earthly father. The concept of a Father God, who is always there, comforted me at a time when I felt very far away from my father. That song became my anthem, and at night—when my stepdad was screaming at my mom and my father was raising his new family in another city—I began to whisper prayers to my Heavenly Father.

As I got older, my stepdad grew increasingly weird and controlling. He seemed especially aggravated by my father, too, and over time, my father was no longer welcome at our house. My stepdad didn't even want to hear my father's name spoken and insisted that we refer to him as "you know who." To make matters worse, my mom never defended my father, even when my stepdad made jokes about him being a foreigner and suggested that he wasn't a "real dad." If he happened to be at home when my father called, I was too afraid to say, "I love you, too" before hanging up the phone. I was also too young to understand that my stepdad was doing more than just being mean. He was purposely trying to create distance between me and my father so I'd be less likely to call on him if I needed to. As it turned out, I would need my father sooner than I thought.

When I was eleven, and while my mom lay in the hospital nursing their newborn son, my stepdad molested me for the first time. I remember feeling shocked and betrayed, even as he promised to never touch me again. A few months later, he did it again, but that second time, he made the mistake of criticizing and comparing himself to my father.

Listening to him bad-mouth my father, especially after what he'd done, enraged me! That anger gave me the courage to speak up before the abuse got any worse and as soon as he left for work that day, the first person I tried to contact was my father. When the collect call didn't go through, I called my mom, who immediately called the cops. But she weakened her position as soon as my stepdad told her I was "confused." My mom had a newborn and a four-year-old to support, as well as a new business to run, so she probably wanted to believe him. She was also worried about people finding out—including my father, whom she feared would "take me away from her" if he knew. When she begged me to tell the police that I'd misunderstood my stepdad's actions, I refused, at first. But she promised me that as soon as she got things in order with the business, she'd make him leave. Frightened and ashamed, I eventually did what she asked. I still regret that decision today.

My stepdad stayed with us for nearly two more years, which was the worst time of my life. Not only did I have to choke down the truth, but I also didn't have the space to heal because my abuser was still living in the house. I walked around in a fog and tried my best to hide my developing body beneath baggy clothes. He never touched me again, but he'd leer at me constantly, which was really frightening. I found myself beginning to fear all men, including my father, who probably wondered why I cringed whenever he tried to hug me.

For two years, I kept that promise to my mom and remained silent about the abuse. But by the time I was thirteen, I couldn't stand it anymore. One day, while my father was driving me to his house for our six weeks of summer, I buried my face in my hands and sobbed out the ugly details of what my stepdad had done to me. As I talked, my father hugged me tight, but didn't say much.

"I wish you'd told me sooner," he finally managed to say.

Then, he called my mom.

Until this day, I don't know what he said to her, but she immediately kicked my stepdad out of the house and eventually divorced him. I felt such a sense of relief, and I was so grateful to my father for rescuing me from what had become a living nightmare. But before the summer ended, I learned that my father was going away, too. He'd accepted a new job in Australia and was moving there with his family. By the time he told me, his plans were already in motion, so there was nothing I could say to change his mind.

For the first time since my parents' divorce, I felt abandoned, and I couldn't shake the awful feeling that I should have been important enough for him to stay. Just before he left, my father gave me a copy of Paul Young's album, *Every Time You Go Away*, and said that the title track was our song. I must have played that song a hundred times over, even as I tried to accept the fact that he was going to be living on another continent.

That first year he was gone, he called and wrote to me faithfully. Sometimes, I'd write back, but I often forgot to mail the letters. It's probably no coincidence that I started dating my first serious boyfriend soon after my father moved away, but I didn't make the connection back then. I became so emotionally attached to my boyfriend that it was like an addiction. If he gave me enough attention, I was happy. If not, I was shattered. What I didn't realize was that I was using him to fill the gaping hole in my heart that was left by my father. It was a pattern I would repeat again and again over the next decade.

I was so consumed with my relationship that when it came time to visit my father in Australia the next summer, I decided that I'd rather stay home to be with my boyfriend. My last-minute cancellation broke my father's heart and put a dent in his checkbook. When I received a letter from him a few weeks later, telling me how much I'd disappointed him, the angry feelings I'd kept buried inside seemed to explode. I immediately wrote him back, using that letter as an outlet for all my pent-up feelings of abandonment. I even viciously compared him to my boyfriend, who "would never leave me, like you did." My father didn't speak to me for months after that. A short time later, he lost his job, which meant he wasn't able to pay for me to visit the following summer. I didn't see him again for three years.

From age thirteen to twenty-two, I only saw my father twice—once at sixteen and once when I graduated college. As usual, he kept in touch through letters and occasional phone calls, but as much as I loved reading his words and hearing his voice, I still missed his hugs, his scent, and his face. Looking back, I regret that I wasted so much time ignoring those empty feelings and telling myself that I didn't need him, even as my aching heart said otherwise.

While my father was on the other side of the world raising his family, my mom became my best friend. She taught me about boys and waited up for me when I came home from my dates. She also took me to church, nourished my Christian faith, and encouraged me to save sex for marriage. My mom is also the one who scraped together money to buy me a car and, when I developed an interest in writing, my first typewriter and computer. When I received an award for winning an essay contest, made honor roll, and graduated high school, I looked into the audience to see my mom's smiling face. But no matter how much I wished he was there, too, my father's face was always missing.

As difficult as it was not to have him around during my teenage years, I didn't recognize that I was looking to other men to ease the pain of missing him. His absence left me feeling insecure, which made me vulnerable to unhealthy relationships. Although I managed to maintain my virginity, I gave too much of myself away to unworthy men. I developed unhealthy emotional attachments and measured my self-worth by how a guy, *any* guy, felt about me at the moment, just as I'd done with my first boyfriend. The end of every relationship—whether it lasted a month or a year—left me shattered. I struggled with depression as a teen and young adult, especially after a breakup. After two breakups in particular—one just after high school and the other, in graduate school—I nearly took my life. The only things that stopped me from committing suicide were the fear of eternal separation from God and my belief that He had a purpose for my life.

My father-hunger issues really seemed to escalate during my twenties. In grad school, I met an older guy who reminded me of my father. I fell head over heels for him, but he was never willing to commit. Although I was never happy in the relationship, I just couldn't let go. When he finally broke things off during our last semester, I sank into one of the worst depressions of my life. Things got so bad that I ended up seeking therapy and taking antidepressants for a few months. During one of my counseling sessions, I admitted to my therapist that when my boyfriend hugged me goodbye, I experienced the same sense of loss and panic I felt every time my father went away. That was the first time I'd ever connected my emotional attachments to my boyfriends with missing my father.

During that awful time, and just after sending him a frantic email about my breakup, my father called to comfort me. He listened to me cry and offered advice. Just hearing his voice made me feel like maybe he was not so far away after all. He and his family had moved to Lebanon by then, and he invited me to come for a visit, "just to get away," but I decided I wanted to finish school before visiting.

With a lot of prayer and help from my family and friends, I managed to graduate with my class. Once I got on my feet and settled into a new job, I took that vacation to Lebanon to visit my father. Along with reuniting with him, I had a chance to spend time with my stepmother and siblings as well as members of my extended family, many of whom had not seen me since I was a baby. My entire family embraced me. To my surprise, I felt a deep connection to the Lebanese culture that I'd never forgotten. Most important, and for the first time in years, I felt connected to my father and his world again, which felt so good.

At the airport, saying goodbye to him was still hard, but I believed my father when he promised me that we'd see each other soon. Before I boarded my flight, he handed me a small gift, which I unwrapped on the plane. Along with a beautiful pen, he'd included a letter inside that read:

Dear Haj Haj:

Here we go again, saying goodbye. I would be lying if I said I felt any different now than I did the first time you left me to go to your mom's 24 years ago. There never seems to be enough time for us to make up for all the lost time, no matter how hard we try.

Somehow, seeing you pretty, confident, and smart gives me the comfort I always needed to survive the thought of being away from you. How you turned out—you make me proud.

All my love, Baba

As I read his words, I began to sob uncontrollably, completely unfazed by the passengers sitting on either side of me. I was amazed that my father could express the same feelings of loss that I felt every time he went away! When I was missing him for all of those years, he was missing me, too. I've read that letter so many times over the years and each time, it helps to ease a little bit more of the pain I felt about being separated from him.

Reconnecting with my father prepared me for my relationship with my future husband, whom I met a year after my trip to Lebanon. By that time, I was communicating with my father regularly and was no longer looking for someone to fill his shoes. What I found in my husband was a partner, not a replacement for my father. Having my father there to walk me down the aisle at my wedding was a dream come true, and watching him become a doting grandfather to my two children fills my heart with joy.

While I am so grateful that my father reached out to take my hand when I reached out for his, I still find myself struggling with father-hunger issues sometimes. There are moments when I can't help but wonder what my life might have been like if I'd grown up with him. Even as an adult, I long for more time and attention than he is able to give, and saying goodbye is not any easier than it was thirty-five years ago.

My healing began when I finally acknowledged how much I needed my father and stopped looking to other people to take his place. I don't know if I'll ever really stop grieving the time we lost, but I'm trying hard to enjoy him now. I'm also learning to forgive both of my parents for the choices they made that hurt me. Ultimately, I've learned to overcome by looking beyond my earthly father for the wholeness I need. For that, I look to my Heavenly Father, because when I felt fatherless, alone, and scared, He gave me a reason to live and have hope. He reminded me that I am *His* child. ∎

III. Deceased

My Daddy's Girl, Still

KIRSTEN WEST SAVALI

MY FATHER, Theodore Joseph "Bubber" West, died on October 18, 2011. In retrospect, that brisk Tuesday morning was cruel in its normalcy, despite the sense of dread that crawled along my spine as soon as I opened my eyes. But no one or nothing could have prepared me for the day ahead.

Barely a month had passed since we'd moved to Apple Valley, California, so I initially chalked up the uneasy feeling to being surrounded by the unfamiliar. Living just enough for the city of Los Angeles had become too much of a financial strain on my family, but I still wasn't quite used to the stillness of the surrounding mountains. Though I tried to comfort myself with that simple explanation, I couldn't shake the feeling that something was . . . wrong.

I asked my husband, Savali, if he knew of anything that happened, or was *supposed* to happen, on October 18. He didn't. Then I remembered that it was the birthday of one of my best friends from college, so I thought that realization might quiet the fear that was snaking through my heart. It didn't.

So, I tried to call my father, in Mississippi.

I've always been a daddy's girl, so picking up the phone to call him was a natural thing. It's something I did several times a day, without thought, just to hear his voice or run something by him or tell him I loved him. He did the same with me, so the call was not an event. My only intent was to ask, "Daddy, what's October 18?"

But he didn't answer the phone.

I tried calling again and again and again and again, but he didn't pick up. I didn't immediately connect my anxiety to his nonresponse, though. Maybe if I hadn't been so distracted by deadlines, I would have. All I felt was annoyance because he knew how much I worried about him. The only reason I didn't call someone to go check on him was because I knew he'd been taking a new medication for high blood pressure that made him sleep heavily. That's why he hadn't been answering the phone regularly during the days prior, so I decided to get some work done and call him back in a few hours.

So, a few hours later, I was home alone working while Savali took our sons, Walker and Dash, out for a walk. I was immersed in my thoughts when I received an email from my stepmother. The email, which came in at 7:12 p.m., shouted at me from the screen—"URGENT: Please call one of us! Mama."

My feelings of anxiety came flooding back, and I immediately dialed her number. She said that everybody had been trying to reach me. At that time, my phone reception was notoriously horrible, so I missed a lot of calls. While trying to contact me, they remembered that I'm always online and checking email, so they tried that and it worked.

"Hey, mom. What's wrong?"

"Hey baby, have you heard from your brother?"

"No, I've been sitting here working and haven't gotten any phone calls. What's up?"

There was a long pause.

"He came home from work and found your father dead."

My world shattered.

I dropped the phone, fell to the floor, and wrapped myself into a fetal position as guttural sounds escaped from my throat. I didn't recognize the sound of my own voice. I was somewhere hovering above my body, gazing down dispassionately at the broken human being on floor, gasping in terror.

Not Daddy.

Not Daddy.

Not Daddy.

October 18. The details of what happened next are a blur—my husband and sons walking in and seeing me on the floor surrounded by fragments of a plate I'd thrown; hearing my stepmother call my name over and over through the phone; my husband wrapping me in his arms—but I remember the shards of pain like it was yesterday. And from that day until this one, I don't really recognize myself anymore. I've come to the conclusion that, in that moment, my heart was hollowed out from the inside, and an emergency mechanism kicked in to keep me alive—kind of like on a parachute. It still functioned as it should, but one more blow and I might not have made it.

I had always been afraid of losing him. My mother died when I was eighteen months old, from a brain aneurysm. They had been a couple since junior high school, and even though the grief of losing the love of his life made my father want to run away and fold into himself, he stayed. He was thirty-one years old then and raising two daughters—me and my eleven-year-old sister—on his own. He would eventually remarry and give me two adorable baby brothers, but in those earlier days, it was just the three of us. He used to tell me that when my sister was asleep, he would allow the tears he'd been holding in all day to stream down his face as he talked to me about my mother and cried it out. He swore that I would look deep into his eyes as if I understood every word. And he laughed when he recalled how I would hit him over the head with my bottle and announce my juice order—"apple juice, light ice"—exactly how I drink it to this day.

Growing up, he was more than just a father to me. He also became a father figure to many of my friends. From elementary school through college, through family trouble, school difficulties, and breakups, he served as a father to many other young women who didn't have one. I didn't realize the void he was filling at the time. He was just Daddy and our house was just the spot. That's the only reality I ever knew.

Daddy made sure that home centered our existence, which is something that remains with me. That's the legacy I will pass down to my sons, too. He believed that when the world is against you, when nothing else is going right, you should always be able to depend on your family. I'll never forget how he made New Year's Eve so special, every year. Rather than going out to parties, I'd be at home, standing in a circle and praying with my family. Though I'm agnostic now, I still smile at the memory of my hand curled inside of his. No matter what I was going through at the time, when the clock struck midnight, he would turn to me and say, "This is your year, Baby Girl."

Though my father was what some people might call over-protective, he didn't just shelter me. He molded me. He taught me the importance of community and made sure I understood my history. He talked to me about the Freedom Riders and the cold-case murder of Wharlest Jackson during the civil rights era. He explained the undeniable fact that integration without education was the worst thing that ever happened to the black community. He sat me on his knee and taught me about the Mississippi State Sovereignty Commission profiling the NAACP as a radical organization. From politics and science, to psychology and business, my father was, and will always be, my blueprint.

Interestingly enough, as my writing on feminism has reached more people, some black men have accused me of being in bed—literally and figuratively—with white men whom, they believe, thrive on emasculating black men. They assume that my refusal to allow the collective fight against racism to distract from my battles against sexism and misogyny means that I didn't have a black father in the home. And they seem genuinely shocked when I tell them that it's quite the contrary: I owe my feminism to my father.

He taught me to never depend on a man for my well-being and to always be self-sufficient. He stressed to me that I should never tolerate disrespect from any man. And he warned me that men would try to possess me—body and mind—and manipulate my emotions. He didn't shame me about my interest in sex, either. Instead, he taught me that my body was sacred and that if I did have sex, I should protect myself and make sure my partner was worth it. Most importantly, he taught me to never allow any man to tell me what I couldn't do, not even him. I owe my life, my being, and my intersectional feminism to the greatest man I will ever know.

We moved back home to Mississippi after his funeral. I needed to be close to the streets he walked, the buildings he entered, and the people he saw. I needed to be under the same corner of the sky, to see the same sunrises and sunsets. That's the only way I could breathe, the only way I could *exist*. With my father's transition, I felt vulnerable to cruel people who would no longer *not* have access to me because of the force field of his love. The thought of coming to town, burying him, and leaving like a relative passing through never crossed my mind. I needed his protection, even in death.

For weeks, I would go to the cemetery, bury my hands in the dirt, and will him to come back. Below that cold ground was my father's body, and if death was the only way for me to be next to him again, then I was open to death being the answer to the numbing grief that, most days, felt too much to bear. These days, some well-meaning people tell me that, by now, I should be feeling better. And to them, I paraphrase Ossie Davis's words about Malcolm X: *Did you ever talk to my father? Did you ever touch him, or have him smile at you? Did you ever really listen to him? For if you did, you would know him. And if you knew him, you would know why "feeling better" is not going to happen.* I know, beyond all reasonable doubt, that if the world could feel my father's energy, *be* his energy, it would be a better place. He was my everything, and if not for the fear and guilt of even thinking about causing my children the same pain that I felt, I'm not sure I would be here today.

When Daddy first died, the pain was a living, breathing thing that encompassed me, owned me, controlled me. Now it's seeped under my skin, into my blood and bones. It's a part of me. I see it in my eyes when I look in the mirror, hear it in my tone, recognize it in my thoughts. It's a shadow that follows me, a lingering chill in the air even when it's warm. That feeling has become something I no longer try to fix because, over time, I've grown to understand that it never goes away.

Besides the bouts of depression and anxiety, another excruciating realization is knowing that I'll have no more pictures of him to comfort me. What I have is what I have. The pictures of him—hugging me, laughing, dancing—that once brought me comfort have become a reminder that time has stopped. His image is frozen. His voice is silent. His body is inanimate and all I have are these *gotdamn* pictures. They will never be enough.

I miss his hands—wide, calloused hands that would rub my back or grab my hand just to kiss the palm and tell me he loved me.

I miss lying across his bed watching a Motown special on television and discussing the "feud" between the Temptations and the Four Tops.

I miss his laugh. Oh, his laugh could light up a room and reverberate for hours after he left.

I miss reaching for the phone to call him in the middle of night, just because.

I miss the light that came into his eyes whenever I walked into a room, knowing that it reflected the light in my eyes at seeing his face.

I miss seeing him get dressed for work in the mornings. I still remember the familiar scent of his aftershave and cologne wafting through his bathroom as I trudged in, blearily, to get ready for school, always passing his watch and ring where they sat perched on his nightstand.

I miss cooking with him after my brothers were asleep.

I miss going to his office and stopping at the coffee machine just outside his door to make him a cup before walking in—cream, two sugars.

I miss the famous card tricks that he'd pull out whenever my friends came over.

I miss dancing with him whenever he slid "My Girl" on the record player or when it came on the radio.

I. Miss. Him. Every second, of every minute, of every day. And the more time that passes, I miss him more.

I don't want to have to "cherish the memories." I still want my daddy to pull up to my home that he's never seen and say, "Hey, Baby Girl!" I want him to be able to go to Walker and Dash's school for Grandparents Day, tell them bedtime stories, and give them too many cookies when I'm not looking. I want to see him laugh and dance. I want to call him and not have to say a word before he says, "What's wrong, Baby Girl?" before telling me the corniest, most inappropriate joke ever, just to get me to laugh.

My laugh hasn't been the same since.

After he died, I spoke with one of his doctors and discovered that he was suffering with chronic obstructive pulmonary disease (COPD). That's what he was covering up when he wouldn't allow his doctors to give me information. I realized that when he sounded short of breath during our phone conversations, it was really because he couldn't breathe. His doctor told me that since his COPD was stage four, he had less than twenty-five percent lung capacity left when he died from a heart attack, alone in his bed, while I was thousands of miles away, wondering why he wouldn't answer the phone. If there was ever a man who deserved to be surrounded by love when he took his last breath, it was my father. That thought haunts me still.

My father always said that he lived a good life, a *full* life, and that all he really wanted to be remembered for was being a good daddy. I can say, without hesitation, that his mission was accomplished. He was my hero, my strength, my best friend, my rock. He is the man by whom all men will forever be measured, and I am so extremely honored to love him and to have been loved by him. Though my world has shifted on its axis, this I know is true: grief is the price one pays for love. I am fortunate to have known my father's love so completely and so intensely, to have had him there to walk me down the aisle at my wedding and to have seen his face at the hospital when I gave birth to my two older sons. I am grateful that he was there to wipe my tears and hold my hand for thirty-one years.

Almost a year after my father's death, I gave birth to my son Reid. Family and friends call him my dad's twin and it's true. From the light in his eyes to the way he tilts his head, he reminds me so much of my dad that my heart aches with joy and pain. More than anything, I wish he was here to play with the grandson whom he didn't have the chance to meet. I wish he was here to let Reid splash in the bathtub until water gets everywhere and, later, smooth the bed and pat his hand on the empty space beside him—my signal to "give him his baby."

Late at night, when everyone's asleep, I find myself talking to Reid and running my fingers through his hair just as my father did with me after my mother died. I tell him that his grandfather would have given him the moon on a string and put the stars in his pockets, just to see him smile. And he looks deeply into my eyes as though he understands every word. ∎

Going There

JENNY LEE

Here are the facts: I am forty-five years old. When I was twenty, my father killed himself during the summer between my junior and senior years of college. His suicide was shocking, but not a total surprise, as he was severely depressed in the months leading up to it.

Nine months to the day after he died, my bipolar older sister hung herself—or so I thought. Her death was less shocking because she'd tried to kill herself many times before. The hanging part was rather unexpected, but then again, she was a true original, and it was so like her to go out with a big ending. A day later, when what was left of our family—me, my mother, and my older brother—met in Memphis, the coroner informed us that the time of death was off and that her live-in boyfriend was in custody. As it turned out, he'd strangled her, then hung her body to make it look like a suicide.

Now *that* was shocking.

I'm going to try to stick to my father here, but since his and my sister's deaths are so tied together for me, it's only fair that you know everything.

Okay, let's say that you and I had a rich, mutual friend who owned a great beach house in Malibu and she invited both of us over one weekend. Of course we'd have this super fun time, but say, after I left early because I'm neurotic about traffic and needed to get home to my dog, you were all like, "Wow, what an awesome chick. She's so warm and friendly and has such charisma." That's when our rich friend would respond, "Yes, she is absolutely all of the above, which is pretty amazing . . . considering."

There is something in the dramatic pause before she says the word, "considering," which would make you stare hard at her. That's when she'd lower her eyes and turn her head to look out at the spectacular view of the ocean. Then she'd tell you everything I just mentioned about my father's and sister's tragic deaths. Upon hearing all of this, you'd be shocked, mainly because, well . . . it's a shocking story. But like most everyone who hears it, you'd find yourself surprised, too, because whatever image you might have of a person who's lived through a Lifetime movie-of-the-week-style personal tragedy, I probably don't fit that image.

I am not in rehab. I am not bitter. I am not exceptionally pro-miscuous (well, I was a bit promiscuous in high school, but that was before all the shit went down). I don't engage in secretive, risky behaviors like shoplifting, or sleeping with degenerate heroin addicts or Republicans. I don't have a gambling problem, though I do enjoy playing the slots in Vegas. I am not in debt. I don't go sky diving, rock climbing, or insert-any-other-risky-adventure-type-of-sport *here,* just so I can feel alive.

Yes, I am divorced, but trust me, the demise of my marriage had nothing to do with my dad. Also, I'm still on good terms with my ex-husband. I do not have children, and while I could probably make a case about how that's not related to past events, I wouldn't be straight-out lying. There might be a little "thou dost protest too much" going on with that one, though. My choosing not to have kids is definitely related to the fact that raging mental illness clearly did not skip a generation in my family.

I'm not saying all of this because I want a trophy for not falling apart after these terrible things happened. I am simply pointing out the fact that I've always been acutely aware of the ways my life could have broken bad given my past circumstances. And sure, perhaps I am a little bit proud of the fact that I didn't end up in a fluffy bathrobe, strolling the grounds of some lush sanitarium in Connecticut while talking to squirrels and other woodland creatures that may or may not be plotting against me.

If there were a big bookkeeper in the sky auditing my life right now, I'm pretty sure he'd crunch the numbers and tell me something doesn't quite add up. I fully believe that there must be an emotional cost to the tragic events of twenty-five years ago, some psychic tax I've had to pay. Sometimes I wonder if I haven't been living as much as *gliding* in a state of denial for all these years. Like maybe I'll open my mailbox one day and all of these past-due bills will come fluttering out. I don't know . . .

I've often wondered if I need an emotional forensic accountant to go over my past and identify all of the places I've tucked away my pain, with the hope that I've conveniently forgotten where I stored it when I was twenty. The problem with this idea is that emotional costs are not numerical, and this stuff is not so easy to figure out. These are warranted fears of mine that I'm not even sure I want to explore. Shouldn't I just hold on to the life I've reined in so tightly and hope for the best? Isn't that my prerogative? Why would I even want to "go there," so to speak? But here I am, "going there." To remember. To contemplate. To wade in and muck about, to see what kind of person I am having lost my father so long ago.

If there's one platitude from my father that I use the most it would be, "If you're going to do something, do it right." He said this on several occasions, like whenever I was tasked with washing his midnight blue 1985 Cadillac Eldorado in the driveway. After I finished, he'd come out to inspect my work, only to discover that I hadn't bothered to wash the hubcaps. Then he'd make me do it again. And, sometimes, again.

This lesson really sank in when he bought a John Deere riding

lawn mower. He called it the "Cadillac of riding lawn mowers."
I, of course, wanted to be that girl who cruised around on it in
my shorts and bikini top, without a care about whether I was actually mowing the backyard. One day, I hopped on and started
going too fast, which meant I wasn't cutting the grass properly.
I wasn't paying close enough attention to the concentric circles I
was making in the backyard, either. Perhaps it was the Tennessee
sun that blinded me, but I didn't see or hear my father jogging up
next to me. Before I knew it, he'd grabbed my arm and scared the
crap out of me. As I scrambled to figure out how to stop the damn
thing, he proceeded to yell at me. I did what any teenage girl would
do in this situation, which is cry in shame. I hated when he yelled
at me, but that day, his chiding worked, because he never had to
say that phrase to me again.

His fatherly lessons have served me well throughout my life,
especially when I think back to the summer I was sixteen, when he
made me get a waitressing job. He wanted to make sure I understood how hard it is to be on your feet for eight hours a day, serving
people for little money and even less respect. His lesson was that
there was a reason he pushed me so hard to get a good education—
he wanted me to be able to make a good living later in life. Although
he did once tell me—during a heinous teen phase that involved
glasses, braces, and a bad perm—that I had to work extra hard
because I wasn't as pretty as my older sister and might have a harder
time finding a husband. Both lessons sunk in, because I now know
how to support myself *and* I'm a really good tipper.

Sometimes I wonder if I have taken all of his fairly generic
advice more to heart because I only have a limited amount of
it. Where others might have their fathers around far longer than
twenty years, I have to make due with all the wisdom he gave me
over that short amount of time and recycle it in every instance
where I could use fatherly advice.

I don't feel sorry for my fatherless self as often as I did when I was in my twenties. When those feelings come up these days, there are a few questions I ask myself. Is it better to have a crappy father for a longer time or a good father for a shorter time? What if I had a father who disappointed me continually, spent my college savings at the track, or cheated on my mom with hookers? Or what if I discovered that he was a supervillain in charge of a massive crime syndicate?

Obviously, I would take the supervillain, because that would mean I could avenge his death while wearing some sexy, slimming spandex outfit in a futuristic movie, knowing that I, too, would meet my end at the hands of some Batman-esque hero. But that would be fine, because I'd get the last word as he was about to kill me by saying in a gravelly voice, "Didn't your dad ever tell you it's not nice to hit a girl? Oh right—you didn't grow up with a dad either." And then I'd die. But after that, I would take the good father for a short amount of time, which is basically what I got.

So, what made him a good father?

First, he provided well for his family. As far as parenting goes, I think if at all possible, you should help your kids get to college, whether financially or by making them go. I'm Korean, so we have a genetic belief in education. He did not abuse me, my siblings, or my mom. He was fairly old-fashioned in his belief that women should do all the cooking and cleaning, but I blame that on misogynistic Asian culture. And most of all, I think he tried hard to be a good person and do the right thing. For example, he was a doctor and would never turn away patients if they couldn't afford to pay. I know being a good person who does the right thing sounds easy, but as I get older I realize it's not. At all.

My dad gave me my first puppy, which was probably the single happiest moment of my childhood. But one of my all-time favorite memories was the time he bought me and my brother and sister baby ducks for Easter. He got them from a pet store and just showed up with them at home. They were a total surprise. When you're a kid, this is huge—like ten thousand times better than a chocolate-filled Easter basket.

He hadn't even told my mom about it, which is probably why she was so pissed. I love that he did this because it was such a bizarre thing to do. Maybe I also liked it because it felt like something I would do, too, so I feel comfort in knowing where I came from. Plus, it's always fascinating when someone does something that is seemingly out of character. Given his normal demeanor—serious, quiet, and strict—showing up with three baby ducks was totally unexpected.

I appreciate this memory all the more now. Not because of the gift itself, but for all that came after it. Think about it—after you give each of your three kids a baby duck, then what? Well, then you have to deal with your angry wife and let her know that *no*, you're not going to return them to the pet store. Next, you have to buy a plastic baby pool at Kmart so the ducks have a place to swim. Then you have to build a little wooden house for them, so they have shelter. Next, you have to buy chicken wire and construct a makeshift fence around said house and pool because baby ducks are actually quite fast and you can't have them running all about your backyard (even though it is hella fun to chase them around).

You then buy two more baby ducks, though this time, you buy wild baby ducks, which are much smaller and fuzzier than the regular white ones with little orange feet you got the first time. (Who knows why these were purchased? Perhaps to appease the annoyed wife, because he'd only bought baby ducks for the children and she felt left out?) So, there were five baby ducks, all living together, and it was hilarious to the kids that the wild ducks were "the parents" and they were so much smaller than the bigger "kid" ducks.

Then you have to explain to your three kids how during a weird Tennessee rainstorm, one of the tiny wild ducks squeezed through the fence and wandered over to the lot next door, which was overgrown with very tall grass and weeds, and somehow that baby duck got lost and died out there. (Maybe this is why I never leave the resort when I go on vacation. *Never leave the resort!*)

This leads to a baby duck funeral, complete with the requisite shoebox coffin, and digging a hole in the backyard at the insistence of your youngest daughter (that would be me). You would try in vain to train the ducks, but to no avail, because they're ducks and really, what can you expect them to do? And eventually, your wife puts her foot down and demands that you do something with these ducks, which are now older and just eat, swim, and shit everywhere. So, you find a local farmer who has a pond and agrees to take them as long as you drop them off yourself. This is when you discover that young adult ducks are more than capable of getting out of a cardboard box in the backseat of your midnight blue Cadillac Eldorado. And as noted before, these ducks are not potty-trained and demonstrate as such on your velvety, midnight blue interior.

After you drop off the ducks, you then have to go home and clean the backseat of your car, dispose of the fence, the kiddie pool, and the little wooden duck house (did I mention that he'd painted it white, too?). What you are left with is an unsightly patch of backyard where all the grass is now dead, which your wife makes you replace immediately because it looks like an alien spaceship has landed in your yard as opposed to a family of four ducks who had lived there for almost a year.

Only later did my father find out that when pet stores sell ducks, they clip their wings, so those ducks really had nary a chance out in the wild and were probably killed by foxes or some other woodland creature very shortly after their arrival at the farmer's pond. He told my brother the news, but he didn't tell me—maybe because he wanted to protect me, because I was crazy about animals.

So, if you were a duck, not a great story. And if you were my dad, then perhaps you got more than you'd bargained for. But as far as I know, he never complained, and in the process, he gave me this unforgettable memory of what a good father would do for his kids. It's a story that is infinitely richer because I am now old enough to know what it means to deal with an unhappy spouse; what it takes to own a house with a big backyard; how maddening and soul-crushing places like Home Depot, Kmart, and landscaping stores are on the weekends; and how precious your free time is when you work your ass off during the week. No, he didn't pull me from a burning building or save me from drowning, but I don't want high drama in my personal life anymore. I am happier with small acts of love.

Obviously, I'll never know if he regretted his more-than-likely impulsive decision to buy us those baby ducks on that random day, because again, he died when I was still too young to understand what a pain in the ass those ducks actually were. But I choose to believe that he didn't regret it. That all the weird, dumb, childish glee those surprise Easter ducks brought us was more than worth all the mundane, annoying tasks he had to do after he gave them to us.

Or maybe that's why he killed himself.

Kidding.

I think that's been the key to me not losing my shit when everything went to hell in my life. Obviously, I had no choice in what befell me back in the early 1990s, and I'm sure it was natural to feel like I was doomed. For a long time, I was convinced that my mom, my brother, and I would die at any given moment, but that feeling has faded over the years. My coping mechanism since then has increased twofold. First and foremost, I have my sense of humor. I'm not suggesting that these deaths made me funny, but I am saying: who knows if I'd be a professional comedy writer without them? In the writers room where I work now, three out of eight of us have suicides in the immediate family. I'm just sayin'.

But more important than even humor has been the idea of personal choice, and understanding that it's within my power to look at every memory of my father, however I need to look at it, for as long as I needed to. Sure there was a lot of rationalizing going on, but so what? Isn't that part of growing up—learning how the world truly works (and being able to handle it), while still trying to be a good person and live a life that's right for you?

I eventually mentioned those ducks to my older brother. He's the one who told me about their gruesome deaths. I realized that he perceived Dad giving us those ducks in an entirely different way—he thought it was careless and unnecessary, and that those untimely duck deaths were on him. My brother has a far different perspective when it comes to my father's suicide, too. There's a lot of anger and resentment there, but to each his own. I have chosen to see the duck situation differently. Maybe it wasn't all that well thought out on my father's part, but he made the best of it, in every way he knew how. That's all he could do, right? That's all I now expect of myself.

When my brother told me about the ducks' fate, I wasn't thrilled to hear it, the same way I wasn't thrilled to hear that Julie, our very first family dog, didn't run away and join the circus like I was told after she bit the gas meter man. But I'm glad I didn't know until I was older and had some perspective on the realities of life. And I am grateful for all of the time I was given to feel protected and safe, to live in a bubble where dogs run away to join the circus and a family of four ducks could build a new life for themselves at a neighbor's pond. That's something my father gave me for as long as he was able to give it.

I understand that maybe he set me free, into the wild, when I wasn't totally prepared, but I accept the fact that this is what he had to do at the time. I understand that my brother is one hundred percent positive that those ducks ended up terrified, and eventually slain—but I believe that we can't know for sure that happened. And like I said before, I choose to believe that maybe, just maybe, they ended up building a pretty okay life for themselves . . . considering. ■

You Did It Your Way

BRIDGETTE BARTLETT ROYALL

H EY, DADDY!
I'm contributing a piece about our relationship to a book on women without fathers. So many days have passed as I've struggled with how to approach this. I'd sit down at my laptop to type or grab a good ol' fashioned notepad and pen to write, but— nothing. Day after day, week after week, I struggled with what I wanted to share.

I pondered so many things. Should I write about how you taught me the importance of family? Or should I write about the way you insisted that Ben take his little sister outside with him, even though we both protested most of the time? "People need to know that Bridgette is your sister," you'd explain.

How did you have the foresight, all those years ago, to know that your insistence would pay off decades later? The unbreakable bond that Ben and I developed as kids was the catalyst for dozens of folks in our community looking out for me—aka Ben's little sister—when he went off to college and eventually left home for good. That was your doing.

Staying connected as a family was a big deal to you, from in-sisting that we sit at the kitchen table to eat meals together to all of us decorating our apartment during the Christmas season. You even bought me a gingerbread house every year. To this day, I don't like the taste of gingerbread, but I looked forward to you bringing home that gingerbread house because it was one of "our" things. Those and so many other family traditions you implemented helped shape me into the woman I am today.

Then I wondered if I should share what you taught me about finances. You always stressed how important it was to save a portion of my weekly allowance in my piggy bank. When the money from my piggy bank was deposited into a bank account every year, you explained how interest was earned. As I got a little older, you taught me the value of not keeping all of my money in one place, too. Even if I only had twenty bucks, you made sure I put some of it in my wallet, some in my sock, and some in my book bag—ha! You taught me that diversification is key—which is exactly how I approach investing today. But back then, I had no idea that you'd learned that tactic while growing up on the tough streets of South Philly and Jamaica, Queens. You figured that if somebody robbed you, they'd get some, but not *all*, of your hard-earned money!

And speaking of money, or lack of it, you and Mommy did a phenomenal job of ensuring that we always felt loved and supported, despite whatever material things we didn't have at home. As an adult, I now appreciate how much hard work and sacrifice it required of our household to keep me in private school, Girl Scouts, piano lessons, and dance class. And when school field trips came up, I always had spending money for snacks and souvenirs.

I wondered if I should focus on how you found a way to expose two little brown kids from a working-class family in Queens—just a stone's throw from the stomping ground of some of New York's most notorious drug dealers—to everything from The Last Poets to Thelonious Monk, with a dash of Karl Marx and Leo Tolstoy tossed in, too. You encouraged me and Ben to ask questions—"There's no such thing as a dumb question," you'd say. You also told us to always hold our heads up high and look people in the eye when speaking to them, whether we were talking to a Fortune 500 CEO or a minimum wage–earning janitor.

How a black man born in segregated Alabama, who was raised up North and never met his father, could become the dad you were to me, is beyond anything I can wrap my head around. The life lessons you shared with us at the kitchen table were priceless—from the stories of your days traveling the world as a Marine to your memories of living in the racist Jim Crow South as an adolescent. You were my first example of how it's possible for a man to possess book smarts and street smarts.

Like most folks of your generation with Southern roots, you and Mommy regularly spewed off sayings and mantras. Some went in one ear and out the other, but many of them I now revisit frequently. Your words have helped me get through some of the most confusing challenges in my career, and even my love life. One of your sayings that is engrained in my head is, "There are three ways to do everything in life: the right way, the wrong way, and the Bartlett way." Although I'm married now and my last name has changed, that message will be with me forever—stay true to who I am, always and all ways.

What you didn't get to share with me were my high school and college graduations. You never had the chance to grill any of my dates before they took me to the movies or to prom. You weren't around to help Mommy give me the birds and the bees talk. You weren't here to teach me how to drive or help me navigate the first-time home-buying process. Although your spiritual presence was definitely felt, you weren't physically present on my wedding day. If God sees fit for me to become a mother, my children will not get to experience your awesome storytelling or your tickling.

This hurts.

Before your untimely passing in 1990, you made your fair share of mistakes. Some of those mistakes I am aware of, and many I am not. I never want to paint a picture of you being perfect—and besides, how boring would that be? What you were to me was a loving, giving, and protective man of many layers. You were funny, too, and along with being a dispenser of wisdom, you were definitely *the* best tickler in the universe. None of that will ever change.

Your last correspondence with me was via a handwritten letter that you penned from your hospital bed. My fourteen-year-old self had no comprehension of just how sick you were. Weeks of chemotherapy, coupled with the debilitating effects of lung cancer, left you very weak and diminished. I just didn't understand all that you were going through.

In the letter, which is neatly folded in a frame behind a picture of us, you wrote that I was your heart and always would be. I never got the chance to respond or thank you for that letter. You took a turn for the worse shortly after writing it and passed away exactly one week later. I always wished we could have had one last conversation, just so I could express my gratitude to you for being the man and the father that you were, but God had a different plan.

Well . . . thank you. Thank you for everything, Daddy. I'm so grateful to have been blessed to be your daughter.

Love always,

BG ∎

Life, After

MAI HUGGINS LASSITER, AS TOLD TO THE EDITOR

I WAS BORN ON December 27, 1968. Twenty-one days later, on January 17, 1969, my father, John J. Huggins, Jr., was killed at Campbell Hall on the campus of UCLA. He was attending a Black Student Union meeting alongside Alprentice "Bunchy" Carter, who was twenty-six on that fateful day. My father was just twenty-three.

Some say they were assassinated, but it's all just wordplay as neither of them are alive. They were both members of the Black Panther Party, which the FBI had characterized, and targeted, as an extremist group. My father was new to the party *and* to Los Angeles. My mother was, too. At nineteen, she was newly a mother, and then newly a widow.

When my parents met at Lincoln University, the country was in a state of complete unrest. Malcolm X had been brutally killed, four little girls had been murdered in the Birmingham church bombing, and the civil rights movement was in full swing. Like so many young people of that time, they wanted to get involved, so they left college, drove cross-country, and joined the Black Panther Party. The repercussions of their decision now represent just a tiny ripple in our country's history, but they created massive waves in my life.

There are still those moments when I'm looking through old

family photos or scrolling through more recent ones, which include my children, and it hits me—there isn't a single picture that
exists of me with my father. If only there were camera phones back
then, right? But really, I'm not too sure my parents would have had
time for taking pictures. They were too busy trying to change the
world and too young to see that death was right around the corner.
I'm sure they thought they'd be able to continue in the movement
until the world had actually changed.

Although I was only three weeks old when he died, there was
never a time when I didn't know who my father was. I always knew
him. When I was very young, his parents and two sisters told me
the stories of his childhood—about the summers they shared, the
way he danced, and the girlfriends he dated. They also read me the
letters he'd written when he was in the Navy during the Vietnam
War. Something else I always knew and understood about my father
was how the last seconds of his life played out.

My father was the youngest of my grandparents' three children.
He was their only son and my grandfather's namesake. His family
was completely devastated when he was killed and in no condition to
travel. My uncle—the husband of one of my aunts—happened to be
in Los Angeles at the time, so he brought my mother and me to New
Haven, Connecticut, by train. My father's body was flown back a few
days later. The funeral was huge, as he was part of a large family and
his parents were well known and respected in the New Haven and
Yale communities. I am told that there was coverage in the national
news and newspapers. It was a big story . . . and a tragic one.

His death, and especially the way he died, was a blow to so
many people, but I can't begin to imagine the stress my mother
had to endure. She was the mother of an infant, she'd just lost her
husband, and fairly quickly, she became the center of even more
turmoil when she was arrested after joining forces with the New
Haven chapter of the Panthers. She was on trial for two years and
held in prison for the entire length of the trial. During that time,

I lived with my grandparents, and my grandmother took me to visit her every weekend. I was almost three years old when her case was declared a mistrial. Because there was a nationwide call for all party members to move to Oakland, my mother and I moved to Oakland. That's where my first real memories are rooted.

Without my father, I straddled the two very different worlds in which he existed—one with my mother and the Black Panther Party, and the other with his family, with whom I spent every summer. Both environments were fully entrenched in black culture, just on different ends of the spectrum. My grandfather was part of a large West Indian family, from Nevis, that settled in New Haven. My father's upbringing, compared to mine in 1970s Oakland, was fairly suburban. While my time on the East Coast exposed me to working-class culture, Sunday church, family dinners, and black mainstream culture, my West Coast experience was steeped in revolutionary thought within a newer culture, one that encouraged the idea of building your own community and included practices like vegetarianism and meditation. I got the best of both worlds.

My childhood consisted of school years spent in East Side Oakland at the Oakland Community School and summers with my father's family in New Haven, New York City, and Cape Cod. Going back and forth to opposite coasts gave me an appreciation for the many layers of life, in general, and of my family, specifically. I compare my experience being raised on two coasts to that of a city kid who goes down South each summer and is surrounded by an extended family unit, then goes back to the fast-paced city life at the end of the summer. Because of the way I grew up, I think I have a pretty decent understanding of people on various socioeconomic and cultural levels.

No matter which side of the country I was on, I was surrounded by a circle of people who mourned my father, deeply, and loved me, intensely. Just as he was adored by his family, he was also an icon of the Black Panther Party. During my childhood, my mother held a high-ranking position in the party and was viewed as a former political prisoner, so she was held in high regard, too. Articles about my parents were often printed in the Black Panther Party newsletter, and since my father's face was printed on posters as well as in the papers, I think I was able to grasp, at a pretty young age, how the man in the pictures and the man of my grandparents' stories were connected.

I'm sure that anyone who has lost a parent at an early age, so suddenly, so *violently*, has felt the love and also the sorrow that their presence can bring about in others. It's something I was able to get used to.

"Oh, I remember when you were a *baby*," someone might say to me. I always sensed another layer of emotion behind their words. It was written all over their faces. For the first decade or so of my life, I was—for many people, I'm sure—a walking testament to my father's brief time here. When someone realized that I was his daughter, they'd hug and kiss and squeeze me, all while tears fell from their eyes. Sometimes I recognized them, but many times, I didn't.

The timing of my birth and his death were so intertwined that it was easy to mark the passage of time since both events. As a kid, I remember doing that math in my head.

Today is my eighth birthday, so that means that he died eight years ago.

Now I'm ten, so it's been ten years since . . .

Growing up in Oakland as a child of the Black Panthers was not always easy or fun. We lived in dorms for most of the week, and then we'd go to our own homes for a couple of days. And my home was always changing. From my earliest memories, my mother and I—and later, my younger brother—moved. A lot. I'm pretty sure we moved every single year. That is not an exaggeration. A new address became second nature to me, like, *Okay, it's time to move.* We lived near Jack London Square, in the Caldecott Apartments, on Lake-shore, off of Grand, in East Oakland, at the top of Fruitvale, and in North Oakland. We were always moving, that's just what we did. In a way, I think I blocked some of it out as a way to protect myself, but as I started getting older, I realized how much I just wanted to be, and stay, in one place. I wanted to feel settled and secure, and I wondered how much more stability having a present father in my life, a husband for my mother, might have provided us.

My summers in Connecticut gave me the stability I didn't have in California. My grandparents lived in the same house, which is still in the family, for more than forty years, and their household and neighborhood were always very stable. I knew what to expect when I was there. Being in New Haven, which is a pretty small city, helped me feel grounded, and it offered a real connection to my father. For whatever reason, most of my friends in Oakland didn't have their fathers at home either, but there was often no place for them to foster a connection, even if their fathers were alive.

Because my father was gone, everybody stepped up and over-compensated. Along with having my grandfather—who, despite our generation gap, was the closest I ever came to having a father figure—I grew up with *four* mothers: my mother, my grandmother, and my two aunts. I remember a time when I'd have to check in with each and every one of them, all the time, and about every, single thing! But I knew that in me, they saw him, and they always wanted the best for me. They wanted me to do well, especially when it came to being educated.

The summer between ninth and tenth grades, like most other summers, I brought my yearbook to the East Coast with me and couldn't wait to show everybody. I was so proud to have been voted as one-half of the cutest couple. I was voted best dancer, too. My grandmother was not amused.

"What about the debate team?" she asked. "What about student government?"

Just the thought of that whole scene still makes me laugh, but she was very serious. She, and much of my father's family, thought I was losing my way, and they were intent on reeling me back in.

I ended up spending the next sixteen years on the East Coast. After I moved East that summer to attend boarding school, my life expanded and I started thinking about what I wanted for myself. The school was in the middle of nowhere, which definitely helped get me focused and thinking about college. I would fly to Oakland to spend the summers. After a few years, a handful of summer jobs, and four years of college, I started my adult life in New York City, where my aunts had lived since the 1960s. I would never return to Oakland to live and didn't move back to the West Coast until I met my future husband and got married. I'm now back in Los Angeles, where my life started in 1968.

I'd grown up knowing that my father died fighting to make life better for black people. I knew that he didn't abandon us. I knew that he didn't get killed doing something negative, nor was he sick. He also died at such a young age that he hadn't made mistakes that disappointed the people in his life. Because my parents were just beginning their lives together when he was killed, my mother always shared with me the good times they'd experienced. She used to tell me how he was the *most* wonderful person and how much she loved him. Even after everything that has happened, she has remained calm and centered. Looking back, though, I don't believe that my father would have stayed in the party for as long as she did, whether they'd remained a couple or not. On her own, she was a member for more than fourteen years and stayed committed far beyond what I thought was the time to leave. In that sense, I believe my life would have taken a different course, but beyond that, I don't really know. It's really hard to imagine what could have been.

Now that I am married, I understand just how important it is to have a life partner. It's about moving forward, together, and motivating each other to *keep* moving forward. As a parent, I've learned how a father fits into a family structure. My husband is a fantastic father and is very much involved in our kids' lives. I now see the value of having two people, two *parents*, under the same roof. It represents a balance that I never had, and I'm so grateful that our children are able to have that experience.

Every January, the Black Student Union at UCLA honors my father and Bunchy with a memorial service. They light candles and talk about the significance of their lives and the work they did for the community with the Black Panther Party. My mother comes down to speak, as do a handful of other former members. My older son came to the event with me in 2015, which was wonderful for us. I've made sure he knows and understands everything that happened in the past, just as my grandparents, aunts, and mother once did for me. My younger son, whose first and middle names are my father's first and last, doesn't know everything, yet. But we talk about my father often, and I tell him a little bit more each time. ■

That Day in April

WENDY L. WILSON

Typically, your last year of high school is supposed to be one of the most remarkable experiences of your life. Finally, you're a senior, and you can relish every moment of that seniority with your best friends while trying not to let nostalgia prevent you from enjoying the moment. You're on the cusp of adulthood, making vitally important choices for yourself for the first time—including what the heck you'll be doing with your life for the next four years. The whiff of freedom and independence that college brings is a constant temptation. You can't wait, and the anticipation of it all guides you from one day to another.

I learned a long time ago that there's nothing typical about my life. My senior year was supposed to be that wonderful adventure. Instead, it proved to be the worst year ever. Feelings of excitement, hope, and happiness were soon replaced by anger, frustration, and grief, and more than twenty years later, they still remain. But I'm working on it.

Like many men, my father was not a big fan of getting an annual physical. In fact, I don't ever remember him actually going to see a doctor. So when my parents sat me down on an early spring day in March to explain that he needed an operation, it seemed like it came out of nowhere. He looked fine. He sounded fine. Things were always the way they had been with the four of us—my parents, married for eighteen years, my younger sister, and myself. I didn't think this operation was that big of a deal until the "C word" was mentioned. That God-awful, heart-stopping word holds so much power.

Today, cancer doesn't necessarily have to be a death sentence, but in 1992, it had such finality attached to it. My father was diagnosed with colon cancer and was told that part of his large intestine would have to be removed, forcing him to wear a colostomy bag indefinitely. Not the best of solutions, but one that he eventually came to terms with, especially since it meant that he would be alive. There wasn't much choice anyway. Surgery was the only option.

My father's surgery was scheduled for a few weeks later. He was home recuperating about a week after that and seemed to be getting better. Things were getting back to the way they had always been, except they didn't. My mother came home on April 8 to find him passed out in our home. My father, my mirror image, my buddy, the love of my life, had died. This was a man who came to this country from Jamaica in the late 1960s, a time during which the island was riddled with political strife and hopelessness. He was engaging, funny, supportive, comforting, and most of all, he was always there. He was present and in the moment. We did things together as a family and alone as father and daughter. He was a hardworking immigrant who loved music, gadgets, sports, and the sweet smell of men's cologne. He dressed well and liked to socialize, but he was also dedicated to his family. He wasn't perfect and never tried to be. It was okay with us because he was ours.

And just like that, he was gone, simply in a flash. I left that morning for school and said goodbye not knowing it was going to be the last time I would see him alive. I remember he was half-asleep when I said goodbye. The last image I have of him alive is seeing him respond with a wave in the dark.

After the tearful, blurry haze of the funeral, the unfamiliar relatives and strangers in and out of our home, and simply trying to figure out how to be a family of three instead of four, we started asking questions. *How could this have happened? How did he die? The cancer had been removed. The surgery was deemed a success. How was it possible that this forty-four-year-old husband and father was now dead?*

In our fact-finding mission, we learned that my father had an irregular heartbeat prior and during his surgery, but his doctors didn't believe it necessary to find another course of treatment. To them, he was just another black man, and we know what the life of a black man means to those who do not understand its precious value. Until this day, his death certificate says, "pending investigation." The investigation was never conclusive. At least if he had died from the cancer or something else more definitive, we would have a reason. My family has never been able to gain true closure on why he isn't growing old with my mother. In fact, I envy those people who can say, "Well, my father died from a gunshot wound or a serious injury." As morose as it sounds, at least they have a reason why.

He died in April. I graduated from high school that June, and then I left New York for a six-week trip to France in July. Initially, I decided not to go on the trip, but my mother insisted, reminding me that my father went with me to renew my passport and he would have wanted me to go. I'd received a scholarship to travel with a group of American students throughout the French countryside and Paris. It was the opportunity of a lifetime and truthfully, even though I didn't want to leave, I needed the distraction. Plus, when I got back, it was time to pack up my life and start college. I was seventeen years old.

We all experience and handle death differently. One thing is for sure, though: time does *not* heal all wounds. It simply puts a Band-Aid over them. I think about all of the things I wish I could have done for him; I think about how he could have avoided surgery if he had just been healthier. All of the "could haves" and "should haves" swirled through my consciousness so often, but eventually they faded. Then came the day in 2003 when I saw blood in my own stool, and suddenly they all flooded back. I thought about keeping it secret. After all, this is not something one, especially a woman, talks about other than in private. But the silence is part of the reason why my dad is no longer here.

Within a few weeks, I saw my doctor and learned that as the child of a parent who was diagnosed with colon cancer, my risk factors are pretty high—meaning there's a big chance I could also be diagnosed with the disease. We decided to do a colonoscopy to be sure that I didn't have cancerous or even benign polyps growing along my large intestine. Back then, patients had to drink this horrible solution to flush everything from their systems. It literally made you feel like a geyser was shooting from your bum. It was a disgusting feeling, and thank God they have since found more civilized ways of cleaning you out.

I remember arriving for the colonoscopy and feeling oddly out of place. At twenty-eight, I was the youngest person there. Even the staff seemed surprised. Typically, colonoscopies are one of those procedures only people fifty and older need. But as I mentioned before, there's nothing typical about my life. Since my father died at such a young age, it was in my best interest to get the test done right away.

After waking up from the procedure, the doctor informed me that there were no polyps and I was cancer-free. Relief immediately sunk in. I've since had another colonoscopy and will need to have the procedure done every five to seven years because of my family history. I'm happy to say, so far, so good. And while I haven't joined any charity walks or sported a dark-blue ribbon on my lapel in support of the fight against colon cancer, I am an advocate for prevention and early detection. I've returned to the "if I knew then what I know now" moments, thinking of ways I could have helped my father through his medical issues. I couldn't help him, so I'd rather have my story be a cautionary tale for someone else. It's absolutely the only reason why I decided to write about him, because my father's death essentially has no meaning. There is no reason why he's gone. But I've realized over the years that I have to find a way to bring meaning and purpose to his death, so I hope I have done that with telling my story.

Even though my senior year was riddled with so many extremes, I found ways to prevent grief from overtaking my life. I have gone on to have a number of professional successes and every time I get in a tough spot, I know who is watching out for me. I know that I've avoided additional pain, hurt, and disappointment because of my father. I know that he's still protecting me in many ways and continues to be the guiding light I need to see me through the present and future.

I think about when we will reunite and when I'll have the opportunity to finally say thank you. He was only my dad for seventeen years, but he left me with such a wonderful impression of what a man is supposed to be, and do, for his family. If I didn't have that, I would have settled for second and third best a long time ago. I have so many things to be thankful for, and having Errol Wilson as a father is always at the top of the list. ■

The Way It Should Be

GABRIELLE REECE, AS TOLD TO THE EDITOR

I BELIEVE THAT EVERYBODY enters the world with a hand of cards. We all get high cards and low cards, so it doesn't really matter if your hand is dealt from a full deck or not. Where you're from or how your life starts out doesn't matter much, either, because it's ultimately up to *you* to figure out which cards to play and when to play them.

Sometimes I think people look at me and make the assumption that I must have had it easy. I haven't. Not at all. While I've enjoyed success as an athlete, model, and author, getting there definitely wasn't easy. I was very fortunate to have the support of many great people during critical times in my life, but I put in a lot of hard work, too. I also played my high cards as often as I could. That's just who I am, but I can admit that parts of my personality were amplified by the environments in which I was raised. I also think part of my outlook is based on not having a dad. Maybe I might have been more inhibited if he was alive. I'll never know.

I was five years old when I saw my father for the last time. It was the summer of 1975 and he'd come to visit me in Long Island, from California, and we went sailing for the day. At the time, I was living with my mom's close friends—whom I still call my aunt and uncle—and I remember the day a few months later, in October, when the call came.

Our house was pretty small, so it wasn't hard for me to hear my Aunt Norette on the phone in the next room. I couldn't make out every word she was saying, but I could tell she was talking to somebody about my dad. The tone of her voice let me know that something wasn't right, but I couldn't imagine what it was. After she hung up, she came to the doorway of my bedroom and told me that my dad had been in a plane crash . . . that he'd passed away.

For as long as I can remember, I've had a strong survival instinct. That could be the reason why I have such a keen sense of understanding of what is happening, or what's *about* to happen, based on hearing a tone or even just a word. Before my aunt came to my doorway that day, I think I was already bracing myself for the shift that was about to occur. Because I'd already had an early experience with separation from *both* of my parents, I think I'd started accepting change, quite matter-of-factly, when I was about three or four years old. There was always a part of me that could take a dose of reality like, *Oh, okay, so this is how things are going to be now? I got it.*

My parents met in California in 1969 and I was born in January of the following year. They tried to make a go of it, but honestly, I don't think they really even knew each other. By the time I was eighteen months old, they'd broken up. Two years later, when I was three and a half, my mom moved to Mexico City, where she was training dolphins, while my dad, who was from Trinidad, stayed in California, where he was in school. Just before he died, in a plane he was piloting, he'd completed his doctorate degree and started teaching. My mom was pretty young and though I'm certain she was doing the best she could, she wasn't really capable of taking care of me then. That's why I was sent to Long Island to live with Aunt Norette and Uncle Joe.

Although I wasn't with either of my parents, I was a part of a stable family unit during the three and a half years that I lived with my aunt and uncle. With them, I got used to having structure. They made sure I had a routine and a pretty regular schedule, which is what kids need. I knew that I had to brush my teeth every morning, and that I'd have my hair brushed up into a ponytail and be walked outside to wait for the school bus. It was those simple things that mattered so much and gave me a base.

I was seven when I went to live with my mother and her new husband, who was Puerto Rican. Moving from the States to Puerto Rico was definitely a shift. Then the three of us moved to the Virgin Islands. Another shift. Although I'd left one family unit, with my aunt and uncle, and entered a new one, with my mom and stepdad, there were huge differences in the way the two households were run. Where I'd been used to routine and structure, my life with my mom and stepdad was much more loosey-goosey. For instance, I remember that during their honeymoon, which lasted about eight weeks, they left me in the care of a neighbor, who, to me, seemed like a random lady they barely knew. That's not something that would have happened in Long Island.

Now that I'm a mother, I have a better understanding of the role of a parent. It's not so much about being in control of your children as it about being in charge. Looking back on those years with my mother and stepfather, I realize just how much I needed to have some order in my life. Because there really *wasn't* any order, I supplied it myself. I was the one who woke them up in the morning. I made the coffee; I found the lost pairs of glasses and misplaced purses. I also made sure I knew where the keys were, so I could run outside to start the car to make sure they got me to school on time. I was an only child, and that became my role in our household. That's just how it was and I got used to it.

My mother didn't really say too much about my father, about their time together before he died, or about how his death had affected our lives. I didn't press the issue with her either. Instead, I think that I became the male and the female in my life. That's not to take anything away from my stepfather, though. He wasn't the most authoritative figure, but I couldn't have asked for a better stepparent. He was married to my mom until I was twelve and was always very kind and loving to me, almost like a friend. After we moved to Florida—where, in eleventh grade, I started playing volleyball and later earned an athletic scholarship—he'd send me a couple of hundred bucks a month, just so I'd have some money in my pocket. He's always been a good guy and these many years later, I still talk to him quite often.

Though I'd long accepted that my father was gone, there were definitely times when I wondered what my life might have been like if he were alive. I also thought about the fact that I never really had a chance to say goodbye to him. Back then, there wasn't any extra money for plane tickets, so I wasn't able to fly cross-country to participate in his funeral services. After he was cremated, it would be my paternal grandmother, auntie, and uncles who scattered his ashes. Because he died that way, so suddenly, I can only imagine how difficult it was for them to let him go.

At eighteen, I started modeling and became independent. That's also around the time that I became very close to my father's family, whom I'd lost touch with over the years. Most of them had moved from Trinidad to California by then, so I'd fly out to visit and spend time with them. I had a chance to meet some of his old friends, too, and I could see how much they all really loved and missed him. I remember how many of them were taken aback to see me, as a young adult, especially because he and I have such similar features. The shape of my face is just like his, as are the shape and color of my eyes. And though I got most of my height from my mother, who is 6'3", he was quite tall, too.

The memories I have of my father became a bit abstract over time. I recall that we had a good rapport. Like most little girls, I saw him as my hero during the short time we had together. In some ways, though, I think death lets a person off the hook a little bit.

Because I was so young when he died, I was never hurt or disappointed by him. Knowing that he was such a well-liked person has allowed me to think of him as a very smart, charming, and handsome man. That's how I've always remembered him.

On the inside of my right ankle, I have a tattoo of a cross. It's a replica of the one he was wearing around his neck when he died. I got that done when I was twenty-two. I have a few pictures of us together, too, but I don't remember those moments we shared. Sometimes when I think of him, he feels like a concept, in a way . . . and the pictures are proof of the concept, that he was once here. I look so much like him, and when I see him in those old photos, I find myself thinking, *Yeah, I did come from somewhere. There is another part of me.*

When I was twenty-five, I met my husband. I was interviewing him for a short-lived cable TV series, and the attraction between us felt like a lightning bolt. It was probably the only time that's ever happened to me. Eight days later, we moved in together. I moved from Los Angeles to be with him in Hawaii. Living five hours apart wouldn't really give us the luxury of being able to catch a last-minute movie together, so it was like, *Are we in or are we out?* We were in and have been married for almost twenty years now.

Like me, my husband was raised on an island and feels a strong connection to culture. Having lived in Puerto Rico and the Virgin Islands, my roots are steeped in Latin and West Indian culture, while he very much relates to Polynesian culture. We both have an appreciation for gathering and food and music because that's how we grew up. Another thing we have in common is that neither of us grew up with our biological fathers. Because he is a man, he processed that void differently, but we definitely have a shorthand and mutual understanding of the experience. We are on the same page about a lot of things. Once we got married, though, I realized just how clueless I was about how to make a relationship work.

Although I'd been privy to marriage in the two households I'd lived in as a kid, I found that I was deathly afraid to commit once *I* got married. I was scared to be open and was constantly holding back from myself and from my husband. He often reminds me of a conversation we had during the early part of our marriage.

"You told me once, 'No one and nothing is above my survival . . . not even you,'" he said. "Do you remember saying that?"

Vaguely.

I must have said it, though. That's exactly how I used to feel.

When I was growing up, and especially after leaving Long Island, I never really felt safe or protected, so when we first got married, I was stoic. Instead of speaking up when something bothered me, I just kept it in and told myself, *Well, this doesn't work for me . . . and that doesn't work for me, either.* That's how I protected myself. I was very strong-minded during our first few years together, but eventually I realized that there is another way. You have to be willing to take a risk, which is something my husband, who's a champion surfer, does all the time in every part of his life. It's something I had to learn to do, along with how to be vulnerable. That takes courage, too.

The truth of the matter is that love of any kind can be messy and inconvenient, but instead of feeling like, *Ick, this is too messy and inconvenient*, you have to show up and show your feelings. I've always been pretty tough, but on the other side of that, I was probably still that little girl who'd lost her father. At five years old, I couldn't know how not having him in my life would affect me in the long run.

Even though I had to wait until my adult life, I think I finally got my fill of what I missed out on. In my husband, I have a very strong male in my life, but our relationship is in no way based on a parental dynamic. He is my partner, first, and he's also my friend. He's not my dad, but he protects me and our family, which I appreciate. I also appreciate that I found someone to love and to be happy and successful with in life. I got what I needed after all.

A good father is someone who cherishes, loves, and adores his daughter and makes her feel perfect the way she is. He represents honor and directness and also teaches her, by example, how to read a situation. And he is protective of her, too.

When I see my husband with our three daughters, I don't think, *Oh my goodness, that's so sweet.* Whether they're talking, laughing, or going back and forth about something silly, it just seems like the way it should be. ■

Death of a Stranger

REGINA R. ROBERTSON

Every man in here has dated a woman with some daddy issues.
That shit ain't fun, okay?
She's giving you a hard time over some shit her daddy did in 1969.
That shit ain't never fun.
—CHRIS ROCK, *NEVER SCARED* (2004)

IT WAS A MONDAY NIGHT. No, maybe it was a Tuesday. Actually, I'm not sure that I remember which night of the week it was, but I was on the phone talking to my mother, about whatever, as we often do. She told me about her tennis game that day, I told her about the latest deadline I was stressing over. The usual. There was nothing different about this conversation we were having, until she paused . . .

"I have something to tell you," she said.

Okay.

Whichever night it was, it was the night she told me that he'd died. She called him by his first name, which was among the short list of things I ever knew about him. What she didn't say was that my *father* had died. We both knew that he was never my father. I'd never even met him, so I didn't really have much of a reaction.

"Oh, okay," I said.

And that's all I said. Then I just listened.

She went on to say that my uncle, who still lives around the way, texted her to say that somebody had texted *him* the news. He didn't elaborate, though, which is so like him. My uncle has always been a man of few words. So, my mother relayed the news to me as it was relayed to her. It was just a statement, nothing more, nothing less.

Oh, okay.

And then our conversation continued for a few minutes more.

My mother and I live on opposite coasts, and since it was getting late back East, we soon said our goodbyes and wished each other a good next day. The next day came, and went, and we spoke again, about regular stuff. Then a whole week went by before I even thought about the fact that she'd told me he was dead. That's when I started thinking about what I felt about this man who was supposed to have been my father.

What came to mind was the seed he'd planted in my head so long ago, the one that had been rotting away since he left. His absence had been my proof that men didn't love their families, which was as true to me as the sky being blue. I knew that a man could walk away and leave a woman holding the bag, holding the bills, *and* holding the baby. Because I'd once been the baby who got left behind, I was always very aware of the possibility. That's just the way I was wired.

One day, I was talking to my cousin, and when our conversation veered to the subject of our intertwined roots, I told her that I grew up believing that men didn't love their families. She was shocked.

"You really thought that?" she asked me.

"Oh, absolutely," I said.

What I didn't tell her that day was how long it took me to try to unlearn that lesson. In some ways, I'm still trying.

Discarded.

That's the best word I can muster to describe the sting of abandonment. Even as a little girl, I knew that men didn't stay. Over the years, I've read articles and studies that suggest that had my father stuck around, he would have been the first man to love, protect, and provide for me. He might have also held my hand and guided me through this unpredictable maze called life and been the model for what I'd later look for in a mate and all of that, but yeah . . . no. He wasn't there, ever, and I was not that girl.

My mother gave birth to me, her only kid, just after one o'clock on a Wednesday afternoon in the winter. The time of my birth is etched into my brain because every year, she calls me at the exact hour, the exact *minute*, that I entered the world, as she refuses to believe that it's actually my birthday until that moment. She started making those calls after I left for college and now that we live in different time zones, she calls me *twice* on my birthday, at the exact time I was born—first on Eastern time, then on Pacific time, three hours later. It's become our ritual. Every year I play along, just to hear her laugh.

She was twenty-two when I was born and for the most part, she was on her own. Yes, my grandmother was there, as were some of her girlfriends, but when she was seven months pregnant, my father—her husband of two years—was out of the picture. He'd left to play basketball overseas—where, exactly, I never really knew. Aside from the abbreviated tale I once overheard about her tossed-in-the-trashcan wedding band, the details surrounding his departure from our lives have remained a mystery. All I ever really knew was that he was gone and he never came home.

I grew up as part of a family unit of four. It was my grandmother, my uncle (who returned from the military when I was a year and a half), my mother, and me. As far as I understood, we were a nuclear family. My grandmother was one of two sisters amongst a close-knit set of five siblings, and as much as my great-aunts, uncles, and cousins were ever-present, it never really dawned on me that everybody else had two sides of their family. I only ever had one.

There was a time when I naively assumed, as many kids do, that everybody lived the same life at home. Then I met my first best friend, who would become my comrade at elementary school and in dance class. We lived in Queens then, and my friend's two-family house was not too far from ours. She lived with her mother, father, older brother—who I had the biggest little-girl crush on—along with her grandmother and aunties who lived upstairs. I hung out at her house after school sometimes, and while I always had fun, being with her family made me realize that *my* family was different. Somebody was missing.

My mother used to make these banana milkshakes. They were just ice, milk, and slices of banana, but to my young palate, those milkshakes were the ultimate delicacy. One night, while she was doing her magic with the blender, I asked about my father. As soon as the words left my mouth, I wished I could have taken them back. She wasn't very happy about my question and asked me why I wanted to know. I didn't have an answer, so the conversation ended right there. Perhaps she was still dealing with her emotions stemming from being deserted with a child. Or maybe, in that moment, she didn't have the words to explain the situation. Either way, I knew not to bring the subject up again.

I'd seen his face in photos. We kept the photo albums in the living room, and I'd flip through them every so often. In one album, there were a few pictures of me as a toddler, sitting on the lap of an older woman whom I knew to be my paternal great-grandmother. She was the only person from my father's family who visited me when I was a baby, and she passed away shortly after those pictures were taken. Then there was my parents' embossed, white leather wedding album. My mother wore this fabulous pillbox hat under her veil, and she looked so young and hopeful. She later told me, laughingly, that she was upset because the August humidity had rung the very *life* out of her press n' curl. My father was tall and slim and appeared to be happy standing by my mother's side and when they smiled for the camera from inside the limo. All in all, it seemed like a good day, but other than my mother's family and a few of her bridesmaids, the latter whom were dressed in warm, yellow gowns, I didn't recognize any other faces. Like him, my father's family were strangers to me.

The summer before I started fifth grade, my mother and I moved to Silver Spring, Maryland. She had repeatedly insisted that New York was "no place to raise a child." I'd heard her talking to her friends about moving, but I didn't believe she'd actually do it. I didn't want to leave Queens. I didn't want to leave my family, my friends, and my dancing school, but my mother was on a mission. After taking a few trips up and down Interstate 95, we packed up our stuff and made the final, one-way trip to Maryland. I remember crying for the entire four-hour drive.

I could feel the stress she carried as she tried to create a new life for us. I remember feeling like it was just the two of us against the world. Looking back, I know that some of her struggles could have been alleviated if she'd had help. I used to wonder if she ever tried to take my father to court, but as I got older, I thought, *Why should she have to?* When I got older, I asked her, only once, if she ever got any financial support from him.

"Not a dime," she said.

It wasn't just about money, though. It was about investing time and energy, which is what my family did. My mother and grandmother did the heavy lifting and my uncle picked up the slack. I knew what my mother had sacrificed for me. She gave up her young adulthood when she became a single parent. She nursed me through my annual bouts of tonsillitis, taught me how to drive, and stayed up all night to help me finish my college applications. My grandmother insisted that I learn how to balance a checkbook and stick to a monthly budget. Always a consummate lady, she also taught me how to apply liquid eyeliner and lip gloss, with a wand! My uncle surprised me with my first bike and years later, when I had issues with my landlord in Brooklyn, I knew who to call. As soon as my landlord saw my uncle step out of the car, he completely changed his tune. I don't think my uncle even *said* anything, and he didn't need to; his presence alone was enough to squash the drama. I remember being so fascinated by that.

Aside from the cues I took from music, television, and movies, I hadn't the slightest idea about how relationships worked in real life or what a man's role was within a family unit. Nor did I have any understanding of how a man should treat a woman, or not. That ignorance could explain why, in junior high, I met a three-years-older guy who wasn't interested in me beyond clumsy, sneaky sex. It was a horrible experience, one that I blamed myself for over and over. How I wished I'd known better. But the fact is, I didn't.

I spent the next few years beating myself up for that misstep, so much so that when a friend asked me to be his prom date, my first thought was, *Why me?* I even proposed the question to him and since I couldn't come up with an answer when he countered with, *Why not you?*, I decided to take the chance. At sixteen, that was probably the first time I realized that I was starting to talk myself out of things. It's something that I have to constantly keep in check, even today.

My grandmother used to tell me that "no man is an island," but it was always very hard for me to believe that. After her mother died, when she was four, my grandmother and her sister and brothers were raised by their father, who made sure that all of his kids stayed together. That was back in the 1930s. I didn't think she understood what my life was like because, for starters, she'd grown up in another time. Also, her upbringing was completely different than mine. I always felt alone—not necessarily lonely, but definitely alone. And I felt invisible, as if I could exist on the periphery without anybody really noticing, which, for the most part, was rather freeing. Some of those feelings stemmed from being an only child, but having one of my parents completely MIA made me feel quite forgettable, too.

Back in the day, there was this happy-go-lucky, frolicking-in-the-grass tampon ad that boasted the tagline, "Out of sight means out of mind." I'd heard that phrase many times before, but there was something about that ad that made me think, *I'm out of sight and out of mind, too.* Since my father left before I was born, he didn't know me, and he couldn't possibly give a shit about me. To him, I didn't even exist. I was a nonfactor. That's when I realized that not only did he nor the rest of his family see me, they weren't thinking about me, either. Or so I thought.

One afternoon, a few weeks before my seventeenth birthday, a woman called the house and asked to speak to my mother. This was before the days of caller ID, and what I remember most about that phone call is that the caller *refused* to identify herself. All she said was that she'd call back later. *Whatever,* I thought, as I went back to whatever I was doing. Hours later, when my mother came home from work, I told her about the mysterious call, but she had no idea who it could be. A few minutes later, the phone rang again.

The woman who called wasn't just some random person. She was my "aunt." She'd sheepishly dialed our phone on my father's behalf to inquire about my age. Although they weren't quite sure how old I was, he—and perhaps his family, too—was hoping that I'd be turning eighteen so that he would be completely, *officially,* off the hook for any child support or some craziness like that. Whatever was going on sounded like complete madness to me and honestly, I don't think I've ever seen my mother so mad. Before she hung up, she asked the caller if she'd even bothered to acknowledge *me*, the subject of her bungled investigation, when she called the first time. She had not.

That phone call was the closest I've ever come to being acknowledged by my father. At that moment, I realized that he was a coward, yet for some reason, I remember feeling embarrassed as hell. Any curiosity I'd ever had about him died on that day. Two decades later, when my writing career was picking up steam, my picture and byline were featured in several national magazines. People were reading my work and watching my moves, including a few from my father's family. There were emails popping up in my mailbox from people I didn't know and had never heard of, which was, and still is, very odd to me. After so many years, why would they want to be in contact with me? What could we possibly have to talk about? I never heard from my father, though.

Even when I was navigating through my teenage angst, I never felt that I lacked self-esteem. I always felt kind of fabulous in my skin and had really big dreams. I was fearless when it came to going after what I wanted for myself, and none of my confidence had to do with needing, or receiving, male attention. While other girls were daydreaming about marriage proposals and the cut and clarity of the diamonds in their future engagement rings, I was in dance class, at pom-pom practice, or somewhere fantasizing about who I wanted to be when I grew up. I always knew that I wanted to follow a creative path, but I never considered painting a husband into my bohemian-styled life portrait. I knew that knights in shining armor didn't exist and that nobody was coming to whisk me away so we could live happily ever after. And really, since the man with whom I shared DNA didn't want to be bothered, it was hard for me to envision another man wanting to, either.

I remember making an annual promise to myself to try to change my outlook on relationships and do better *next* year. When I was nineteen, I bargained, *Oh, by the time you're twenty, you'll have figured it all out.* Then twenty became twenty-one, twenty-two, and twenty-three. But I never quite figured it out. There were good guys and those who weren't necessarily good *for* me. There were also a few who lied, for sport, then lied on top of their lies, which is something I could never tolerate. But no matter who I was with or for however long, I always kept one eye open and one foot on the ground. I never wanted to swing too far off my axis. Sometimes I was successful; other times, not so much. I blamed myself for everything that went wrong—even after some of the men from my past reached out to apologize for *their* part in what went wrong. As much as I appreciated their words, I still thought it was me. I felt like I'd been cursed.

I never knew what to expect from a man, nor was I ever quite sure when I should back off, move on, or simply step aside and let him to take the lead. Surely I'm not the first woman to sit by the phone while willing it to ring, or to ignore my instincts about choosing the wrong man, but it always felt like such an exhausting exercise. It felt like I was constantly starting over from the beginning, and for me, the beginning meant that men don't stay. No matter how sweet everything seemed at the start, I was always bracing myself for the day when the other shoe dropped. It always did. And I always felt like shit afterwards.

I've watched as many of my girlfriends bounced back from bad relationships and were able to be open to a new experience soon after. I just couldn't fathom that kind of resilience. Sometimes I still can't. Then there were women who seemed to manage their relationships with expert precision. I was impressed, but I also knew my limitations. I hated being stuck in a perpetual cycle of wanting and waiting, hoping and wondering, so I started to let go. I needed to catch my breath. Even now, I take breaks between relationships. Some breaks have been longer than others.

"I can't believe you're single," people have said to me.

Others have asked, "Why don't you have a man?"

Not to answer a question with a question, but is there really a proper way to answer that question, especially for someone who doesn't *obsess* about having a man? There's another question that I'm often asked by those men who frown upon me when they feel I'm thwarting their attempts to open doors and pay for dinners.

"Why won't you let a man do what a man is supposed to do?" they ask.

That question always stops me in my tracks, but I usually just laugh it off. How do you explain to someone you've just met that for so long, you didn't really *know* what a man is supposed to do?

It was actually one of my male friends who showed me, by example, what a man should do, especially as it relates to his family. A few months after his first son was born, I joined him, his wife, and the baby for an afternoon in the city. As soon as we got out of the car, he unsnapped the baby from his car seat and bundled him up in the stroller because it was cold outside. He then proceeded to push the stroller down the street while his wife and I walked behind him. What he did is something that many parents do every day, but I was so struck by him in that moment because he was just so *into* it, so committed. He wanted to be there, and he continues to be a great father. When it comes to fathers and *daughters*, I am always taken aback when I see former President Obama with his two girls. He loves them so much, and even when he carried the weight of being the leader of the free world, you could see, in them, that he's always got their backs. I am in awe of that.

As the years go by and I blow out more candles on my birthday cakes, I realize how far I've come. Even when times got hard, I stayed the course and fought for my dreams, but I know there's not much balance in my life. In many ways, I'm still that six-year-old girl who wanted to do so much when she got out into the world. While I'm thankful to have achieved a lot of what I set out to do, I've done most of it by myself. That's how I envisioned it when I was a kid. But I have often wondered if there's something more. I also wonder if there is someone out there who will take this walk with me and want to stick around for the long haul. Maybe he was out there all along, but I didn't see him. Maybe I just wasn't ready.

By now, I am fully aware of the ways my father's absence contributed the warped view I've had of life, and myself. That part has to be over, though. It has to be. Now that he's no longer alive, I don't feel any differently about him than when I was growing up. My father never existed in my life, so in many ways, he was always dead to me. Whoever he was, wherever his spirit might be, my wish for him is the same as for any other stranger who has transitioned. I hope he had a peaceful journey and that's about it.

As for the bitter seed that he once planted in my head, I've spent years trying to dig it up and cut off the weeds that stemmed from it. As a grown woman, I know that I can no longer factor his absence into my outlook on life and love, men and family. While I often wish I'd come to this place a long time ago, I am learning to forgive myself for allowing so much time to pass while I tried to make sense of it all. I did my best, with the tools I had, but I realize just how much I cheated myself along the way, too.

I deserve better. I always did. Somehow, some way, and some day, *soon*, I will get it figured out. I owe that to myself. ∎

Acknowledgments

CREATING THIS BOOK has been a labor of love, one that has taken shape over the course of fifteen years. These pages would not have seen the light of day without the constant support and belief of so many.

First, I'd like to extend an infinite amount of gratitude to my agent, Claudia Menza, for supporting my idea, lighting the path, and keeping me focused when I lost my way—a *few* times! I tip my hat to Jimi Izrael for introducing me to Claudia and also, to my comrade with whom I share a last name, Gil L. Robertson, IV, who led me to Doug Seibold at Agate Publishing. Doug, your kindness and above all else, your *patience*, are beyond measure. There is a method to my madness, and I thank you (and your team!) so much for understanding.

To Valerie R. Robertson, my "madre/padre" and everything in between—thank you for loving me, molding me, and supporting any and every idea that has ever popped into my head. You made me who I am, and I *am* because of you—period. To my uncle, Al Farnell, the epitome of cool, calm, collectedness—see, I really *did* have a plan all along!

I pay heartfelt homage to my late grandmother, Jeanette G. Farnell, as well as to my late great-aunts and -uncles, Eddie and

Lia McClean, Ruby McClean Blake, Clarence McClean, Russell McClean, and Uncle Desmond, and my cousins Renato, Billy, and Debbie Johnson (the latter with whom I share a birthday, whose voice I still remember), Betty and Barbara McClean, and Doreatha Pitts. And to the branches of our tree—David and Renee McClean, Mario "Butchy" Johnson, Carmen Moran, Delores Farrow, Tavio Johnson, Danielle Johnson, Todd and Simone I. Smith, Renato Johnson, Jr., Dolores Pitts, Tyrone Pitts, Charon Torain, Kimmie McClean, and all of my "little cousins" who aren't so little anymore—remember that we are all reflections of each other.

Mad love to my squad who've opened their homes, picked up the tab, and/or lent a shoulder to cry on (and an ear upon which to vent, often!). Bottomless thanks go out to Brooklyn's Finest—Daniela Roebuck, Keisha Lewis, Carolyn Williams, and the late Cornelius Freeman—Rio Cyrus, Courtney M. Anderson, Jabali Hicks, Caralene Robinson, Tiffany Smith-Anoa'i, Stacy Spruill, Brickson Diamond, Arthur Lewis, Hau Nguyen, Cara Donatto, Brennan J. Williams (and Will C.), Fernita Wynn, Rusty White, Greg Braxton, Vivian Scott Chew, Semedra Thomas-Fields, Kim Bishop, Karu F. Daniels, Bridget Bland Bogee, Teodora Mojica, Cherish Cullison, Scott Caudill, and Cliff Warren, my bestie from way back. To my comrades and *very* early draft readers, Nicole Shealey and Calida Garcia Rawles (who also created the cover illustration, using her youngest daughter as her muse—hi, Siena!), I can't thank y'all enough for your eyes and your honesty—like, *seriously*. And to Rodney Shealey, my brother from another, thanks for offering your signature brand of support in the form of a single, powerful sentence—"Just write the damn book!"

To my family friends who've embraced me from the beginning—Ms. Marie West and her clan, my on-the-block family—the late Mr. and Mrs. Bewley, Donna, Michelle, Debbie, Cindy, Eileen, and Charlie—the McKetneys of Queens, the Vervins of Macon, Joyce Mosso Stokes of Washington, DC, my mom's ace-boon, Barbara

Harley, and the Butlers, with whom I go way, way back, to where 140th Street meets 116th Avenue, right across from Ajax Park. Many, many thanks to Dwight, Ben, Tony, the dearly-departed, Alfred, and the entire Butler family for allowing me to share your matriarch's story. I was, and still am, so honored that Ms. Butler trusted me to document her life. To my sister-cousin-friend, Cooky—oops, I mean, Cassandra Butler Jackson—thank you for leading the charge.

Heartfelt thanks are due to my *Essence* family, past and present, for extending me the editorial equivalent of an endless sunny day (and the occasional, *painful* all-nighter!)—Vanessa K. De Luca, Rose-marie Robotham (a lovely woman and gifted wordsmith who has *the* greatest initials!), Wendy L. Wilson, Janice K. Bryant, Bridgette Bartlett Royall, Patrik Henry Bass, Akkida McDowell, and Harriette Cole, who was the first to welcome me into the fold many moons ago. A very special "OMG, Thank You!" to Jeannine Amber and asha bandele for allowing your amazing, whip-smart daughters to share their stories in this book. And to Cori Murray, the fairest, most honest, and supportive editor/partner-in-Hollywood-crime a girl could ever ask for, you are supremely appreciated.

I humbly salute Nelson Boyce for introducing me to Denene Millner, who, as features editor at *Honey* magazine, assigned me to write my first national story, "Where's Daddy?" which sparked it all. A special shout goes out to Tresa L. Sanders, who congratulated me on that story, then proceeded to tell me hers—another spark. Tresa, thank you for those hours-long talks and endless email chains.

I'd like to acknowledge a few folks who've helped me along the way and likely didn't realize just how much—J. Bernard Alexander, III, Motisola Zulu, Cheryl Boone Isaacs, Nancy Bishop, and Jill Motaman. I appreciate each of you for so many reasons. I must also give credit to the writers and visionaries who keep my creative spirit afloat and continue to inspire—Debbie Allen, Anne Lamott, Marita Golden, Shakti Gawain, and Joan Didion. Much respect is also due to the late, great Langston Hughes, who penned my favorite poem, "Harlem" (aka "A Dream Deferred"). I ponder those verses nearly every day.

Boundless thanks and bow-downs are due to Joy-Ann Reid for crafting the beautiful words that open this book. Collaborating with you was a joy (pun intended!), and I'm so honored to have worked with you. Sarah Tomlinson, *your* book spoke so loudly to me that I just had to reach out. Thank you for responding to my note, scheduling that one phone call, and contributing a wonderful piece. It was my absolute pleasure to work with Gabrielle Reece, who was always on my wish list and said "Yes" on the strength of one blind email. Gabby, I so appreciate you and I thank you for understanding my mission. Many, many thanks to Suzanne Gluck and Amy Hasselbeck of WME Entertainment as well as Winsome N. Reid, Clio Seraphim, and Jennifer Meredith Castillo for all of your help—*truly!* And finally, I must say THANK YOU (yes, in ALL CAPS) to "queen" Regina King for just being so dope and down, from the beginning, and for taking the time to edit your story while taping *two* shows and winning Emmys! You are true royalty.

And last, but certainly not least, to Niko Amber, Demetrea Hardiman (many blessings to her mother, Renee Ellis, who passed away during the publishing process), Danielle Rene, Nisa Rashid, Tamala Merritt, Cindy M. Birch, Kyra Groves, Alysse ElHage, Kirsten West Savali, Jenny Lee, and Mai Huggins Lassiter (along with her mom, Ericka Huggins, and aunts, Joan Huggins Banbury and Carolyn Huggins): I really can't think of the proper words to express how grateful I am to each and every one of you for taking this journey with me and sharing your stories with such heart, honesty, and boldness. Thank you for your time and for trusting me *and* the process. I am so grateful to all of you for having the strength and courage to tell the truth. I know it wasn't easy, but we did it! ■

About the Contributors

NIKO AMBER lives in Brooklyn with her mother and her little dog, Bubbles. In her free time, she enjoys reading, baking, and spending time with her grandparents. "The Birthday Present," which she wrote at thirteen, is her first published piece.

DEMETREA HARDIMAN was born and raised in Los Angeles. A lifelong, award-winning athlete, she plays professional tackle football for the Pacific Warriors. She works with the Department of Public Safety at the University of Southern California and is earning her bachelor's degree in sociology. She dedicates her essay to her late grandmother.

DANIELLE RENE is an inspirational writer. She considers herself Southern, but has fallen in love with Brooklyn, New York. A graduate of the University of North Carolina at Chapel Hill, her articles have appeared in several online publications including *MadameNoire*, *The Huffington Post*, *Clutch*, and *For Harriet*.

NICOLE SHEALEY is a native Texan, raised in Massachusetts. A graduate of Chamberlayne Junior College in Boston, she lives in the suburbs of New Jersey with her husband and two sons. "A Lesson from My Mother" is her first published essay.

DESNEY BUTLER (1932-2011) was a native of Brooklyn, New York, and later resided in Queens and Washington, DC. A beloved childcare provider for nearly six decades, she retired in 2007 and spent her free time with family and traveled as often as possible. Her husband, Benjamin

F. Butler IV, and son Wayne preceded her in death. She was survived by sons Dwight, Ben, Alfred, and Tony, and a host of grandchildren, great-grandchildren, nieces, nephews, and dear friends.

SIMONE I. SMITH is a proud wife, mother of four, entrepreneur, and decade-plus cancer survivor. A native New Yorker, she is co-owner and designer of three jewelry collections—Simone I. Smith, SIS, and Amore—and donates a portion of proceeds to the American Cancer Society. Along with earning 2013's Rising Star Award from the National Association of Women Business Owners–Los Angeles, she has appeared on *The Talk*, *Entertainment Tonight*, and *The Insider*, and her designs have graced the pages of *Essence* and *InStyle*.

SARAH TOMLINSON is a Los Angeles–based writer. She received her BA in English, with a focus in creative writing, from Bard College, and her MA in journalism from Northeastern University. She has ghostwritten twelve books, including two uncredited *New York Times* bestsellers. Tomlinson's music criticism and essays have appeared in publications including *Marie Claire*, *MORE*, *Publishers Weekly*, *Salon*, the *Los Angeles Times*, and the *Boston Globe*. Her memoir, *Good Girl*, was published by Gallery Books (Simon & Schuster) in 2015.

NISA RASHID is a student at Brooklyn Friends School in New York City. Her first published work appeared on *The Huffington Post* in August of 2015 when she was fifteen.

TAMALA MERRITT has been an educator for two decades and currently teaches fifth grade. A native of Oklahoma, she earned both her bachelor's and master's degrees from Saint Louis University, with concentrations in psychology and African American studies, educational psychology, and special education, respectively. By her own admission, her life is centered around her family. A proud football mom, basketball mom, *and* cheerleader mom, she lives in Missouri with her husband and three children.

REGINA KING is an Emmy Award–winning actress whose credits span three decades. In addition to her film and television roles in *Jerry Maguire*, *Ray*, *The Boondocks*, *24*, and *American Crime*, she has added director and producer to her resume. To date, King has directed episodes of *Scandal* and *Being Mary Jane*, as well as *Southland*, on which she starred for five seasons. She also helms the production company Royal Ties with her sister Reina.

CINDY M. BIRCH is an award-winning actress, writer, producer, and director. A native of New Jersey and graduate of Rutgers University, she is founder and director of The Short Film Awards (affectionately known as The SOFIES) and cohelms the full-service artist management firm She Boss Entertainment Group.

KYRA GROVES is a Los Angeles–based, multihyphenate creative artist. When she's not acting, writing, painting, or drumming up her next animation idea, she is likely off doing cartwheels in the grass. "The Friendly Demon" is her first published work.

TRESA L. SANDERS is CEO and founder of TreMedia, a full-service public relations, marketing, and branding agency based in New York and Atlanta with a roster of sports, entertainment, corporate, and nonprofit clients including Interscope Records and HBO, among others. She also serves as talent executive for TV One's original series, *Verses and Flow*. She was recognized as part of *Billboard* magazine's Power Panel for 2013.

CORI MURRAY is the entertainment director for *Essence* magazine. Along with wrangling celebrity talent and writing and editing cover and feature stories, she has served as a cultural critic on CNN, E!, NPR, OWN, and BET, to name a few. A graduate of Hampton University, she calls Brooklyn home, though she'll always be a Southern girl at heart.

ALYSSE ELHAGE is a freelance writer and editor of Family-Studies.org, the blog of the Institute for Family Studies. She formerly served as associate director of research for the North Carolina Family Policy Council and as associate editor of *Family North Carolina* magazine. A graduate of both Covenant College and Regent University, her articles have been published by *Acculturated*, verilymag.com, aleteia.org, and ibelieveinlove.com.

KIRSTEN WEST SAVALI is the senior writer for TheRoot.com, whose commentary explores the intersections of race, social justice, religion, feminism, politics, and pop culture. A 2015 recipient of the Harry Frank Guggenheim fellowship, her writing has been featured on *The Huffington Post*, *Salon*, *DAME*, *Clutch*, EBONY.com, xoJane.com, alternet.org, TheGrio.com, and more. Her work is studied in several college courses across the country, she has been cited on CNN and MSNBC, provided commentary on NPR's *Beauty Shop* with Michel Martin and on the *Tom Joyner Morning Show*, and has appeared as a featured guest on Fusion's *Alicia Menendez Tonight* and RT's *Watching the Hawks*. She currently resides in Mississippi with her husband, their three sons, and their Bichon Frise.

JENNY LEE is a television comedy writer and producer who has worked on Freeform's *Young & Hungry*, Disney Channel's *Shake It Up*, and *Samantha Who?* She is the author of the Harper Collins middle-grade children's novel *Elvis and the Underdogs* (and its sequel!) as well as a few collections of humor essays, including *Women Are Crazy, Men Are Stupid* and *What Wendell Wants: Or, How to Tell if You're Obsessed with Your Dog*. She currently lives and writes in Los Angeles with her giant black Newfy, Gemma, and her very tall husband, John.

BRIDGETTE BARTLETT ROYALL is founder and editor of BlackBridalBliss.com, an online wedding planning resource launched in 2010 and named among the top wedding websites by *Essence* magazine in 2014. A Fashion Institute of Technology graduate, she is the former research chief at Essence.com and has contributed to publications including *Delta Sky, Juicy, Essence, People,* and *Real Simple.* A native of Queens, New York, she enjoys traveling, watching *House Hunters* marathons on HGTV, and spending time with loved ones.

MAI HUGGINS LASSITER is raising two boys who, one day, will become amazing fathers themselves.

WENDY L. WILSON is an award-winning journalist who's held the position of managing editor at both *Ebony* and *Jet* magazines. She served as news editor at *Essence* for nearly a decade and also held positions at *George*, *InStyle*, and *Teen People*. A graduate of Skidmore College, she earned her master's degree in journalism at New York University. She is at work on her first book.

GABRIELLE REECE, a former beach volleyball player, fashion model, and television host, is a fitness expert and coauthor of the *New York Times* bestsellers *My Foot is Too Big for the Glass Slipper: A Guide to the Less Than Perfect Life* and *Big Girl in the Middle*. She has graced the covers and pages of *Elle, Shape, Fitness,* and *ESPN* magazine, among others. Reece splits her time between California and Hawaii with her husband and three daughters.

About the Editor

REGINA R. ROBERTSON is the west coast editor for *Essence* magazine. A graduate of the Fashion Institute of Technology, she's enjoyed a career of finding and thriving in her passions, ranging from fashion and music to film and the written word. She has appeared as a featured guest on NPR, *The Real*, KTLA-TV, Centric, TV One, and Reelz, among others, and has been quoted in the *Los Angeles Times*. Born in Queens and raised, in part, in Silver Spring, Maryland, Robertson became a woman in Brooklyn and found her voice in Los Angeles. This is her first book.